Lobster
❤ Lover's ❤
Cookbook

Brian M. Coffey

Evelyn,
Bon Appetit !
Brian Coffey

DOUGLAS CHARLES PRESS
N. Attleboro, Massachusetts

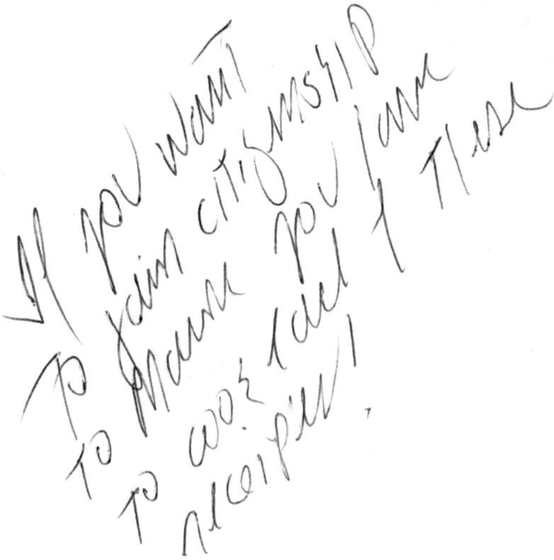

ISBN 0-924771-87-9

Douglas Charles Press
7 Adamsdale Road
North Attleboro, MA 02760
(508) 761-7721

10 9 8 7 6 5 4 3 2

CONTENTS

Introduction

Cooking Methods

Soups, Stocks and Bouillons

Appetizers

Sauces

Salads

Brunch

Tomalley

Entrees

Stuffed Entrees

Crepe Entrees

Dishes with Lobster

About the Author

Introduction

ABOUT LOBSTER

The name lobster originated from the Latin word *locusta*, and the Old English word *loppestre*. The lobster is found all over the world. The genus *Homarus* has quite a variety of species, all basically having five pairs of legs, including two front claws, and antennae. The *Homarus Americanus,* also known as the American lobster, is truly the "King of Seafood." It can be found on the Atlantic coast from Cape Hatteras to the shores of Northern Labrador. However, the largest numbers of inshore lobster are caught along the coast of Maine, southwestern Nova Scotia, and along the southern Gulf of the St. Lawrence. The majority of lobsters are landed by inshore fisherman, but there has been a dramatic increase in the numbers of lobsters landed from offshore fishing grounds, which extend from Georges Bank, east of Cape Cod, to the Chesapeake Bay.

The lobster is usually found on rocky bottoms and in heavily vegetated areas inshore. It avoids direct light as much as possible, living in burrows, mostly staying undercover as much as possible. The lobster is very sensitive to temperature, and becomes very sluggish in extremely cold water.

The lobster's feeding habits are basically nocturnal (night time) and omnivorous (eating both animal and vegetable). Unlike other crustaceans the lobster, being a scavenger, is attracted to decaying flesh by means of its keen sense of smell. Remains of mussels, brine shrimp, crabs, clams, other lobsters, worms, fish, eel grass and sea urchins have been found in lobster stomachs. During the soft-shelled stage of its life, the lobster eats a lot of mussel shells and shrimp cuticle, using the calcium to grow a new shell for itself.

The difference between male and female in the texture and flavor of a lobster's flesh is evident. The female lobster also possesses a delicious band of flesh in her head that the male lacks. The bright orange coral known as "roe" is only found on the female. It is very rich and delicious, even though many people are afraid to try it. When the female is in her reproductive period the flesh is soft and mushy and not as desirable as when she is not reproducing. It seems to be a general rule of the sea that during the reproductive period the condition of a sea creature's flesh is poor. Many fish exhaust themselves during spawning; some even find it fatal, like the eel and the salmon.

The only way to tell the difference between a male lobster and a female lobster (who is not reproducing) is to turn them on their backs and look at the little swimmers on the underside of their tails. The first pair of swimmers closest to the body on the male are very hard and bony, while on the females they are soft and feathery.

Generally, lobsters are dark greenish-blue in color, but infrequently the color can be vary to bright blue, sea green, red and even yellow, due to genetic differences. I was once diving off the coast of Marshfield, Massachusetts, in an area called Beatle Rock when I saw a yellow lobster—the first and last one I ever saw.

Many experiments have been done including tagging to find out if lobsters migrate or not, and for the most part they do not. They are very territorial. An occasional tagged lobster has been found to travel as far as 150 miles, but this is unusual.

As the lobster grows it must shed its hard old shell for a new larger one so that it may continue to grow. This process is called "molting." An entire new shell—carapace, claws, antennae, mouth parts, gills, stomach and eye casings—grows under the old shell. As soon as the new shell is completely formed, nutrients to the old shell are cut off; the shell becomes brittle and cracks between the carapace and the tail under the pressure of the additional growth. While lying on its side in a V position the lobster pulls itself out of the old shell.

After molting, the lobster absorbs water and bloats itself to normal size. Consequently, the flesh is very watery for at least two weeks or more.

Growth varies but it is estimated that lobsters grow about 14% in carapace length and 50% in weight after each molt. The lobster is very vulnerable during and immediately after molting; its shell is extremely soft and the lobster moves very little. It hides under rocks or in its burrow, and as a result the lobsterman's catch is usually small during a period of peak molting, which is usually July through September.

Mature males usually molt once a year, unless they are very old and slow growing. Mature females carrying eggs do not molt, skipping a year, since the shedding would cause them to lose their eggs. Lobsters mate soon after the female has molted; the male is usually hard-shelled. Almost two years can pass between mating and hatching.

Depending on her size, the female will lay between 9,000 and 50,000 eggs. All female lobsters are potential egg producers; however, most females do not become sexually mature until they are at least 90mm (3-9/16 in.) in length. Since about 80% of all lobsters caught are between 81mm (3-3/16 in.) and 90mm (3-9/16 in.), most females do not have a chance to reproduce.

The size of the American Lobster has been dwindling for centuries, and so has the quantity. In the early 1600s historians have stated that five and six foot long lobsters were reported in the waters off the coast of New York. There is proof that lobsters grew to be amazingly large. One now hangs in the Museum of Science in Boston, Massachusetts, with a record weight of 42 pounds, caught off the coast of Virginia.

Around the same time in Plymouth, Massachusetts, lobsters were so plentiful they used to wash up on the beaches in clusters two feet high. At that time the lobster was so common that the early settlers used to crush the dead lobsters that washed up on the beach and put them in their fields for fertilizer. In 1622 Governor William Bradford of the Plymouth Plantation apologized to a group of new settlers because all he could offer them to eat was lobster.

In the early 1840s commercial lobstering began in the state of Maine, and there the fame of the "Maine Lobster" took shape. In less than one decade, lobsters were being shipped all over the world. In 1885 the American lobster industry produced 130 million pounds of lobster, but in three decades the industry had declined to 33 million pounds. Today, with conservation efforts, the industry produces 80 million pounds a year, with 20 million caught in the state of Maine alone.

Despite the fame and tremendous market the American lobster industry has, Canada's is even greater. The Canadian lobster industry is the largest lobster industry in the world. The popularity of this one crustacean is so great that you can find it in every corner of the globe from Sitka, Alaska, to Johannesburg, South Africa.

THE LOBSTER BOAT

by Dick Perkins

Aye, look to her grace as she rides the swell
In fine form like a cherub on a cloud;
With lines of a nymph and pose of a queen
Aye, wherein could so fine a boat be seen....
Ye old shipwright, with skill, crafted her well,
"Mate, can't ye feel to salt sea she's endowed';
Ne'er 'gain will men see such a jewel on the wave—
Aye, those trade secrets he took to the grave.
A lamb now in sorrow, far from acclaim
'Midst the marsh where shrill sea-terns are nesting;
Once proud in her glory, time called her name,
Planks adrift from spruce hull, she is resting;
But I see her proud on the bounding main
With an AYE that is true to her blessing.

Permission to reprint granted by author.

LOBSTER MEMORIES

I have had many truly wonderful experiences with lobsters. They are memories I will have the rest of my life.

In the summer of 1972 I was having trouble finding friends who liked to scuba dive, so I taught my best friend Billy how. My parents owned a small wooden boat and every Sunday during the summer Billy and I would go diving. We would pack up the boat with all the necessary gear, food, cooking equipment and beer that we needed.

We had our favorite spots where we knew there were lots of lobsters. One was a small cave off the coast of Scituate, Massachusetts, a cave that had never seen a lobster trap because it was on the side of a large rock the size of a three-story building.

I was always fascinated by lobsters and how mysterious they could be. The best thing about diving was that we could find lobsters in much better places than traps just by snooping around the ocean floor. We looked for areas with a rocky shoreline, which usually meant a rocky bottom with lots of vegetation and marine life, a haven for the lobsters.

We'd anchor the boat and overboard we'd go, down, down, down, to an environment so beautiful it is hard to put into words. There the lobsters would be, lurking about in dark places, being very cautious whenever they moved. They are shy and extremely unpredictable. When they sense danger they swim for cover as quickly as they can.

When they swim they go backwards, thrusting with their tails to propel them to safety. To catch them, you have to sneak up on them and grab them from behind. You really have to be quick. Billy would hold the mesh bag while I stuck my hand into some pretty dark places to get them.

We would hunt the waters until we either ran out of air or reached our limit. Then we'd go back to the boat and head for land so we could cook the beauties as quick as we could. There is something about cooking lobsters right on the beach in sea water that makes them extra good. If we had the time we'd dig a few clams before we ate so we could have a real feast.

I'll never forget one day we were on a spit of beach at the mouth of the North River eating our lobsters, the ones we had just cooked over a fire made from driftwood. There we were, two kids with no money and a small boat that leaked, eating lobsters and clams on the beach, envied by every big boat that passed us by. Those lobsters were so good that day! It is one experience in my life I think of often and will never forget.

HOW TO BUY LOBSTERS

Lobsters live in the wild and, depending on their environment, come in many different colors. The most common color is a greenish-brown with an orange underside. There are, however, some very rare ones that are blue, spotted yellow or red and some extremely rare ones that are white. I have seen and caught many off the coast of Cape Cod that are blueish in color. Do not be alarmed by their living color because they all turn red when you cook them (except the white ones). Lobsters must be bought alive and so are usually kept in tanks of salt water, sorted into four different sizes. The most common size is 1-1/4 pound.

It is illegal to keep lobsters under a certain size. Some states (Maine, for example) have both a minimum and a maximum legal size. Lobstermen use a gauge to measure from the eye socket to the end of the body shell, called the *carapace*. The legal minimum length of a lobster's carapace is 3-8/32 in. Lobsters smaller than this measurement are called "shorts." The maximum length (in Maine) is 5 in.; they are called "jumbos." Some states (like New Hampshire and Massachusetts) have no maximum length: you can go to a fish store there and buy lobsters the size of a small dog.

Here is how lobsters are classified:

Culls: missing 1 claw, 1 lb to 1-1/4 lb

Chickens: 3/4 to 1 pound

Quarters: 1-1/4 pounds
Large: 1-1/2 to 2-1/4 pounds
Jumbo: over 2-1/2 pounds

Something else you should know: In the summer and fall you can buy either hard-shell or soft-shell lobsters, because every year at those times they shed their shells in order to grow, a process called molting. Before the lobster sheds its old shell it forms a new soft shell underneath the old hard one. For the lobster to get out of its old shell it must split the carapace (the body shell section), and allow the skin between the tail and the carapace to open. The lobster then pumps itself up by taking in sea water, which enlarges the soft shell. The old hard shell then splits off. The lobster at this point in time is very vulnerable. His exoskeleton is paper thin, so he hides until the shell becomes harder. As the shell hardens he goes looking for food and the bait in the traps is usually very alluring.

There isn't as much meat in a soft-shell lobster as there is in a hard-shell of the same size. That is why soft-shell lobsters are a lot cheaper. The meat in a soft-shell lobster has more fluids, which makes the meat softer and not quite as delectable as the hard shell. The hard-shell lobster is a little more difficult to shuck, but a little extra labor yields a far more enjoyable feast.

You will also find that "culls" are a lot cheaper than lobsters with both claws. For many of my recipes I purchase culls because all I want to use is the meat and do not care if they have one claw or two. The majority of meat is in the tail anyway, so unless I am presenting the whole lobster in its shell I go with culls.

Cooking
Methods

There are basically six different ways to cook a lobster—boiling, steaming, grilling, baking, broiling and sauteeing. The most common, and often argued as the only way, is to boil them. I will admit the best lobster I ever had was one that I had caught myself scuba diving and cooked on a beach in ocean water and seaweed over a driftwood fire. Being a true lobster lover but not native to the great state of Maine, I find great enjoyment in preparing lobster in a variety of different ways.

BOILED LOBSTER

(4 lobsters, 1–2 average)

PROCEDURE:

In a 10-qt stock pot pour 6 qt of water. If you are a purist using ocean water, add 1/4 cup of white vinegar. If you are using regular tap water, add 1/3 cup salt. Bring water to a fast boil and plunge the lobsters into the water head first. Bring water back to a medium boil and cook 8–10 min.

If you like to use a lot of different recipes calling for lobster and do not want the lobster to be fully cooked, because you are going to cook it again in another recipe, only cook the lobsters for 4 min in the boiling water. This will cook them enough to make them easy to shuck, and slightly undercooked so that they may be cooked again without making them tough.

SPICY BOILED LOBSTER

(4 servings)

This is a great way to cook lobsters, especially when you are going to let them chill and eat them cold. The meat is cold but the flavor is hot. Old Bay spice mix is made in Baltimore, Maryland, and I use it all the time. It is great for boiling all kinds of shellfish, and can be purchased in any supermarket.

INGREDIENTS:

6	qts	water
1	bottle	beer
3	cups	Old Bay spice mix
4		1–2 lb lobsters
1	tbsp	salt

PROCEDURE:

Place water and salt in a 6–8 qt pot and bring to a boil. Place lobsters in water for 1 min to kill them. Remove lobsters from water, crack claws and cut through the underside of the tail between the swimmerettes. Make cut about 2 in long. This will allow the spices to get inside the meat. Add spice and beer to water, stir and boil. Place lobsters in spicy water and bring to a boil. Turn heat down so the water is on a slow boil and cook 8–10 min. Remove lobsters from water and chill.

I like to serve these chilled and in the shell with a variety of different sauces. They can also be served hot with drawn butter right from the stove.

STEAMED LOBSTER

(4 servings)

This method of cooking produces a very juicy and moist meat. The key is keeping the water boiling as fast as it can.

INGREDIENTS:

4		1–2 lb lobsters
1	qt	water
3	tbsp	salt

PROCEDURE:

In a 10-qt pot pour about an inch of water and add salt. Place something with holes in it in the bottom of the pot so that the lobsters never actually touch the water. I use a perforated pie tin, but anything with holes will do. I have even seen people use a hand grater, one of those square ones, in the bottom of the pot. You can also use a lobster steamer, or any large steamer.

On a high heat bring the water to a fast boil and add the lobsters to the pot. Cover and cook 10–12 min, shut heat off and let stand for 5 min.

GRILLED LOBSTER

(4 lobsters, 1–2 lb average)

This method is great if you are doing a lot of barbequing, and it will impress your friends, but be careful you don't overcook the lobsters. They will dry out and get tough.

PROCEDURE:

Place the lobsters on their backs. Use a large chef knife to sever the spinal cord by cutting through to the back shell where the body and tail are joined together. Then cut the lobsters in half lengthwise. Remove the small sac below the head and discard. Then remove and place in a small bowl the orange roe and the tomalley. Remove and discard the intestinal vein running from the stomach sack to the tip of the tail.

Using a pastry brush paint the shell and exposed meat of the tail with olive oil and sprinkle with salt and pepper. Place over hot coals, cut side down. Grill the lobsters on both sides, brushing ocassionally with oil to prevent the shell from burning. Keep an eye on the tail; do not let it overcook or the meat will be tough. Depending on how hot your coals are, the cooking time is 12–15 min.

In recipes calling for a body stuffing you will need to wrap the lobster bodies with a lightweight aluminum foil to contain the stuffing.

BAKED STUFFED LOBSTER

(4 lobsters, 1–2 lb average)

This is a very popular method of cooking for restauranteurs because it can be prepped ahead of time and kept refrigerated. If you are serving a baked stuffed lobster as an entree at a dinner party, you can get it set up and then go change into your dinner attire.

PROCEDURE:

Place the lobsters on their backs. Using a large chef knife sever the spinal cord by cutting through to the back shell where the body and tail are joined together. Then cut the lobsters lengthwise, down to the back shell but do not go through the back shell. Remove the small sac below the head and discard. Remove and discard the intestinal vein running from the stomach sack to the tip of the tail. Fill body and inside of tail with desired stuffing and drizzle with butter. Set lobsters on baking sheet and brush the entire shell with drawn butter. Bake at 375°F for 18–20 min.

BROILED LOBSTER

This method is very similar to the procedure for grilled lobster. Have a lot of drawn butter on hand before you start; you will need it to keep the lobster from drying out.

PROCEDURE:

Place the lobsters on their backs. Using a large chef knife sever the spinal cord by cutting through to the back shell where the body and tail are joined together. Then cut the lobsters in half lenghtwise. Remove the small sac below the head and discard. Remove and discard the intestinal vein running from the stomach sack to the tip of the tail. Keep the orange roe and the greenish gray tomalley intact. Brush heavily with butter and sprinkle with salt and pepper. Put lobster halves on broiler rack and broil in a preheated broiler 10–12 min, brushing frequently with butter.

SAUTEED LOBSTER

(4 lobsters, 1–2 lb average)

This method of cooking calls for the raw meat to be removed from the shell.

PROCEDURE:

In a 10-qt stock pot bring to a boil 6 qts of water. Plunge lobsters head first into water for 1 min and remove from water. This kills the lobster in a very humane way but leaves the meat almost totally raw. This particular method should be used in any recipe calling for raw lobster meat. Never just cut into a live lobster to remove the meat without killing it first. Remove all meat from tail and claws, along with tomalley and roe. Set the amount of raw lobster meat aside that you need for your recipe.

There are many different ways to saute but the basic procedure is the same. In a saute pan place the desired amount of butter or oil and heat to medium high. Cut lobster into bite-sized pieces and add to pan. Stir constantly with wooden spoon. Toss lobster in saute pan for 2–3 min. Remove from heat.

Soups, Stocks and Bouillons

NEW ENGLAND BOUILLABAISSE

(8 servings)

Bouillabaisse originated in the small seaport town of Marseilles, France, now a very large city on the Mediterranean sea. The tradional recipe calls for a variety of seafoods not available in New England, so I developed my own version. I use the same format in preparation, and conform to the classic recipe pretty closely, with only slight variations. This soup makes a wonderful entree. I like to serve it with homemade croutons, aioli and freshly grated Gruyere cheese.

INGREDIENTS:

1/4	cup	olive oil
2	ea	sliced leeks, white part only
1/2	bulb	fennel, chopped
1	tbsp	minced garlic
1	cup	finely chopped celery
1	tsp	ground black pepper
1		bay leaf
1/4	cup	chopped parsley
1	pinch	saffron threads
1	cup	tomato concasse
4		chicken lobsters
2	cups	mussels, washed and debearded
1	lb	U-15 shrimp
2	dozen	cherrystone clams
2-1/2	qts	cold saffron lobster stock *(see recipe)*
1	loaf	French bread cut into croutons and toasted
1	cup	aioli
1	cup	grated Gruyere cheese

PROCEDURE:

I suggest you make the saffron lobster stock a couple of days in advance. Then this recipe is easy to put together and does not seem so time-consuming.

25

In a large stock pot, heat the olive oil over medium high heat. When oil is hot add leeks, fennel, garlic, celery and black pepper. Cook until soft but not brown, then add bay leaf, saffron, parsley and tomatoes, and cook another 2 min. Cut the lobsters in half lengthwise and place in pot along with all other seafoods. Cover with cold saffron lobster stock and bring to a boil. When the soup comes to a boil reduce heat to a very slow boil and cook another 2–3 min. Remove the bay leaf. With a slotted spoon transfer the seafood to four individual large platters and then cover the seafood with the broth. Serve with the croutons covered with aioli and Gruyere cheese.

Another way to serve it is to put the croutons all dressed with aioli and cheese in the bottom of a soup bowl, cover them with broth and then shuck all the seafood and add it to the soup broth. This is my favorite way to eat it. This is also my all-time favorite soup. I know you'll *love* it.

LOBSTER VICHYSSOISE

(1-1/2 quarts)

This is my favorite summer soup. I love it best with some fresh-baked French bread with sweet cream butter and a nice, cold glass of wine.

INGREDIENTS:

4	cups	peeled and cubed potatoes, 1/2" cubes
2	cups	chopped leeks
5	cups	chicken stock
1.5	tsp	leaf thyme
1	tsp	black pepper
1/4	tsp	white-wine worcestershire
2	tsp	Dijon mustard
2	cups	all-purpose cream
1.5	cups	lobster meat cut into small bite-sized pieces
1/4	cup	chopped parsley
1/4	cup	chopped scallions

PROCEDURE:

In a small stock pot, bring chicken broth to a boil. Add leeks, potatoes, thyme, pepper and worcestershire sauce. Bring to a boil again, cover and let simmer for 1 hr. Remove from heat and drain off one cup of the liquid. Puree rest of mixture in food processor or blender. Add cream to each batch you puree. On the last batch you puree add mustard. Place pureed soup in container and add lobster meat, mix thoroughly. Chill for four or more hours. Serve in chilled bowls, top with parsley and scallions.

27

OYSTER AND LOBSTER STEW

(4–6 servings)

INGREDIENTS:

1.5	lbs	cooked lobster meat
1/3	cup	melted salt pork fat
2	cups	julienne onions
1	cup	julienne green peppers
1/2	cup	scallions
1/4	cup	chopped parsley
1	tbsp	paprika
1	tbsp	minced garlic
1.5	cups	tomato concasse
2	cups	lobster stock
2	cups	tomato juice
1	tsp	black pepper
1/2	tsp	Worcestershire sauce
24		raw oysters
1	lb	freshly shucked lobster meat
1/2	cup	sherry

PROCEDURE:

In a medium-sized pot, heat pork fat until it starts to smoke, then add onions, peppers, scallions, chopped parsley, garlic and paprika. Cook over medium heat until mixture has softened, about 10 min. Stir occasionally. Add tomato concasse, lobster stock, tomato juice, black pepper and Worcestershire sauce. Cover and cook over low heat for 30 min. Add oysters and sherry and cook 5 min more on medium-low heat. Cut lobster into bite-sized pieces and add to stew. Cook 2 min more on medium high heat and serve. This stew is great with some crisp French bread, ice-cold sweet cream butter, and a nice cold glass of white wine.

LOBSTER AND
MUSSEL CHOWDER

(1 gallon)

This recipe is a crowd-pleaser. Watch how many times they come back for seconds. This is a full-bodied chowder oozing with flavor. Make sure you have plenty of common crackers around for this one; you're going to need them.

INGREDIENTS:

5	oz	salt pork, cut into 1/4" cubes
3	cups	minced onions
1/2	tsp	worcestershire sauce
1	tsp	black pepper
1	tsp	leaf thyme, fresh if you can get it
1/3	lb	butter or margarine
3/4	cup	all-purpose flour
1.5	qts	scalded milk (180°F)
1	tbsp	Dijon mustard
5	cups	lobster stock
4	dozen	mussels, debearded and washed
4	cups	peeled and cubed potatoes, 1/2" cube
1	lb	fresh shucked lobster meat
4	tbsp	lobster toamlley
1/2	cup	fresh chopped parsley
1/4	cup	chopped scallions

PROCEDURE:

In a medium-sized skillet, heat cubes of salt pork over medium high heat, stirring occasionally. (The use of salt pork in chowder is an old New England tradition.) When all the fat has melted and you are left with small golden brown cubes of crisp fat, remove the cubes from the hot fat and save them for later. Add onions to hot fat and stir, cook for 1 min, then add black pepper, worcestershire and thyme. Stirring occasionally, cook until onions are translucent. Remove and let stand.

29

In a 2-qt sauce pan, melt butter and, using a wire whisk, whip in the flour until smooth. Simmer 5 min. Add the hot milk and whisk vigorously until sauce is thick and smooth. Add dijon mustard and blend thoroughly. Keep on very low heat so bottom of pan does not burn.

In a 10-quart stock pot, bring to a boil the lobster stock, add mussels and bring stock to a boil again. Boil 5 min. Remove mussels from stock and add potatoes and bring to a boil again. While potatoes are cooking shuck the mussels and discard shells. Cut the lobster into bite-sized pieces. When potatoes are cooked all the way through, add milk sauce, onions, lobster and mussels to stock pot. (Caution: do not overcook potatoes; they turn to mush in a chowder.) Gently stir and blend all ingredients. Add the chopped parsley, blend thoroughly and serve. Top with chopped scallions. Old-time New Englanders take the cooked cubes of salt pork that are hard and crisp and add them to the chowder before they eat it. This sure does make it good! Give it a try.

Note: Chowder tastes a lot better the second day than it does the first. If you can, make the chowder the day before you are going to serve it. Mom always said it was better the next day.

LOBSTER GAZPACHO

(4 servings)

INGREDIENTS:

2	tbsp	stale white bread crumbs
1	tbsp	olive
1	tbsp	red wine vinegar
4	cups	tomato concasse
1	cup	tomato juice
1	cup	diced cucumber, peeled and seeded
1/2	cup	diced yellow pepper
1/2	cup	diced green pepper
1	tsp	chopped shallot
1	tsp	chopped garlic
1/2	cup	diced zucchini
1/2	cup	chopped red onion
1		scallion, sliced
1/4	cup	lobster fumet
1	lb	freshly shucked lobster meat
1	tbsp	ground almonds
1		egg yolk, finely chopped
1/4	cup	chopped parsley
		salt and pepper to taste

PROCEDURE:

Soak the breadcrumbs in oil and vinegar for about 1 hr and set aside. In a large stainless steel bowl place all vegetables and spices and toss gently. Add tomato concasse, tomato juice, lobster fumet, and lobster meat; mix thoroughly. Salt and pepper to taste. Finally, add soaked bread crumbs, ground almonds, and chopped parsley. Chill for 4–5 hr. Serve in chilled bowls garnished with finely chopped egg yolks.

Note: For those who like a spicy hot gazpacho, try adding some Durkee Red Hot Sauce.

LOBSTER STEW

(4 servings)

A New England classic.

INGREDIENTS:

1/4	lb	whole butter
4	2-lb	lobsters
1/4	cup	lobster fumet
1	qt	all-purpose cream
1/2	tsp	paprika
		salt and pepper to taste

PROCEDURE:

Slightly undercook the lobsters, about 6 min. Shuck meat from shell and save tomalley. Cut the meat into bite-sized pieces and place tomalley in a small bowl.

In a large sauté pan, melt butter under moderate heat. Add lobster meat, tomalley, fumet and paprika. Stir and gently cook in butter 1–2 min. Add cream and simmer for 20 min. Skim off any impurities and serve immediately.

BASIC LOBSTER STOCK

(2 quarts)

I use stock to make soups, sauces and bouillons. Stock is an essential part of lobster cooking, and can be kept frozen and used only when needed. Save the shells each time you eat lobster. Made into stock, they can make your next meal taste really great.

INGREDIENTS:

2	ea	carrots, cut in half
1	ea	celery stock, chopped
1		large spanish onion, chopped
8–10	ea	lobster bodies and shells, crushed
2	ea	fish heads and bones from a non-oily fish such as cod or haddock (optional)
1/4	cup	coarsely chopped parsley
1	ea	bay leaf
1/2	tsp	salt
1/2	cup	white wine
1/4	tsp	thyme leaf
1/4	tsp	black pepper
1	ea	lemon cut into halves
1	gal	water

PROCEDURE:

In a 8 or 10-qt stockpot place all the ingredients and bring to a rapid boil, reduce heat to a simmer, cover and cook for 1 hr. Skim occasionally to remove impurities. Remove from heat, strain stock through a chinois or colander, and discard shells, bones and vegetables. Return liquid to stock pot and reduce by one half. Store in refrigerator for 4–5 days, or freeze for up to 6 weeks. It is important to crush or chop all body shells to yield the maximum flavor.

COURT BOUILLON

(1 quart)

INGREDIENTS:

1		large carrot, peeled and chopped
1		large onion, peeled and chopped
1	stick	celery, chopped
10		black peppercorns
2		bay leaves
1	sprig	thyme
3	sprigs	parsley
2	whole	cloves
4	cups	water
1	tsp	salt
1	cup	dry white wine

PROCEDURE:

Put all ingredients in a pot and bring to a boil, and boil for 15 min. Reduce heat and simmer for 45 min. Strain into bowl and discard vegetables, reserving liquid.

LOBSTER FUMET

Fumet is a very concentrated bouillon used to add extra flavor to soups, sauces and butters.

INGREDIENTS:

3	tbsp	olive oil
4–6		lobster bodies & shells, crushed and chopped
1	lb	fish bones (optional)
1/4	tsp	saffron threads
2	tbsp	hot water
4	cups	diced tomatoes
1	cup	diced leeks
1/2	cup	diced carrots
1/2	cup	diced celery
5	each	large garlic cloves, minced
1/4	cup	chopped parsley
1/4	cup	leaf thyme
1	gallon	water
1	cup	white wine

PROCEDURE:

Heat olive oil in a very large saucepan over medium high heat, add the lobster bodies and shells, fish bones if any, and cook for 10 min, stirring occasionally. Mix saffron with hot water and stir until water is yellow, and add to saucepan. Then add the tomatoes, leeks, carrots, celery, garlic, parsley and thyme, cook 2–3 min longer. Add the water and wine, then bring to a boil, reduce heat and simmer for 1 hr. Strain and season with salt and pepper.

LOBSTER BISQUE

(4 servings)

This is a classic New England soup, rich in flavor and in heritage. I highly recommend that you serve it with lobster toast.

INGREDIENTS:

2	1-lb	lobsters, cooked
4	tbsp	clarified butter
1	med	onion, minced
1	lg	carrot, minced
1	tsp	chopped garlic clove
1	stalk	celery, minced
2	tbsp	flour
1/2	cup	dry sherry
1	cup	lobster stock
1	tbsp	tomato paste
1	ea	bay leaf
1	sprig	fresh thyme
1/4	cup	brandy
2	cup	heavy cream
1/4	tsp	paprika
		salt and pepper to taste

PROCEDURE:

Remove all the lobster meat from the shell, including the tomalley. Place in bowl and chill. Chop lobster shells as fine as you can. Heat a medium-size sauté pan until hot, and add butter. When butter starts to smoke, add shells, reduce heat and cook shells for 1–2 min, tossing the shell fragments frequently. Add all the minced vegetables and garlic, and cook for another 5 min. Slowly sprinkle in the flour and cook another 2–3 min. Transfer everything to a 2-qt saucepan and deglaze the sauté pan with the sherry, adding everything to the saucepan. Heat the mixture until hot and slowly add the lobster stock so that the soup thickens, and add the tomato paste, thyme, bay leaf, and paprika.

Reduce heat and simmer for 1 hr. Take all the chilled lobster meat and chop it, place it in the sauté pan and add the brandy. When it becomes hot remove it and run it through a food processor until mushy. Run the soup through a china cap to strain shells, place the soup back in the saucepan, add the lobster and add heavy cream. Bring to a simmer for 20 min. Add a pinch of cayenne pepper and serve.

Appetizers

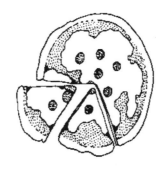

LOBSTER CROQUETTES

(4–6 servings)

Croquettes were first created in a French kitchen. In the mid 1950s they became very popular in the U.S.A. The name derives from "croquer," which means to crunch. The reason for their great popularity is that they're crunchy on the outside, tender and delicious on the inside. They are also very easy to prepare. This is a great recipe for any leftover lobster that you might have after doing a lobster bake, or when you just like to prepare a unique light appetizer.

INGREDIENTS:

1/4	cup	butter or margarine
1		shallot clove, finely chopped
1	tbsp	flour
1	cup	all purpose cream
1	lb	fresh shucked lobster meat, chopped
1/2	tsp	black pepper
1	pinch	garlic salt
1	pinch	celery salt
2		eggs, well beaten
1/2	cup	flour
2	cups	fine cracker crumbs
2	cups	frying oil

PROCEDURE:

In a medium-sized saucepan, melt butter under medium heat and add shallot clove. Cook until slightly brown, about 2 min. Add the flour, blend until pasty and cook until it starts to bubble. Add the cream and blend with a fork until smooth and thick. Add the lobster, black pepper, garlic salt and celery salt, mix thoroughly. Cook 2 more min and add 1 beaten egg. Mix and place in food processor, run motor for 30 seconds. Remove and chill. Shape the cooled mixture into cylinders or cones. Add 1 tbsp of water to the other

41

beaten egg to make an egg wash. Roll them in flour, dip them in the egg wash and then in the cracker crumbs, place them on wax paper and chill until they are firm again. Heat frying oil to 350°F. Place croquettes in hot oil and fry on all sides until golden brown. Remove from oil and allow to drain on paper towels. Serve them hot with the sauce of your choosing (see *Sauces*). My favorite is hollandaise.

Note: These little creations are quick and fun to make. Serving them with different sauces makes them really delicious. A few suggestions on sauces—croquettes taste great with salsa, roasted red pepper, mustard sauce, bearnaise or hollandaise. This mixture will also last several days under refrigeration.

GRILLED LOBSTER AND PESTO PIZZA

(4 servings)

I love to cook outside, probably because I love the outdoors. One of my favorite ways of entertaining is a backyard barbecue. I especially like this recipe because the way the pizza dough is cooked is on the charbroiler. The key to having perfectly cooked dough is not burning the dough when you grill it, so make sure the grill is not too hot. I am also against the use of charcoal bricquettes when grilling outside. I prefer hardwood coals. This is quite exotic pizza, although the hardest part of making it is the dough. Once you've got that down, the rest is easy.

INGREDIENTS:

1		pizza dough *(see recipe next page)*
1/2	cup	yellow cornmeal
1	lb	fresh shucked lobster meat
4		ripe tomatoes, sliced 1/4" thick
1	cup	sauteed mushrooms
1	cup	chopped scallions
2/3	cup	pesto sauce
1	cup	grated mozzarella
1	cup	grated provolone
1	cup	coarsely grated parmesan cheese
4	tbsp	olive oil
1/2	cup	chopped parsley

PROCEDURE:

Divide the dough into 4 pieces and roll each piece into a 6 inch circle. Stretch each circle another 2 inches by hand. The edge shoud be slightly thicker than the center. Brush one side with olive oil and place that side on grill and cook until the dough puffs up. When the charred marks appear remove from heat. Sprinkle cornmeal on the side you oiled.

43

Place the four pizza doughs on a large sheet pan with the grill marks up. Next cover each dough with sliced tomatoes. Cover tomatoes with the lobster, mushrooms and scallions. Drizzle the pesto sauce over the pizzas evenly. Mix all three cheeses together and then cover pizzas evenly with the cheese. Drizzle olive oil over the top of the pizzas and then sprinkle with paprika. Place sheet pan in a preheated oven at 500°F. Cook until cheese is completely melted, about 6–8 min. Remove from heat and serve.

Pizza dough

1	pkg	active dry yeast (1/4 oz)
1-1/4	cups	warm water
1/2	cup	olive oil
1	lb	unbleached all purpose flour
1/4	cup	white cornmeal
1	tsp	salt

Soften the yeast in the water, let stand 5 min. Stir in oil, then add the flour, cornmeal, and salt. Mix all together. Flour a flat surface and knead dough until smooth and elastic, 10–15 min. Wrap in plastic film and refrigerate for 1 hr.

LOBSTER QUENELLES

(4 servings)

INGREDIENTS:

2	1–2 lb	lobsters, raw meat only
2.5	tbsp	milk
1	dash	cayenne pepper
3⁄4	tsp	salt
6	tbsp	unsalted butter
1⁄3	cup	flour
3		egg yolks
1		egg
1	pinch	nutmeg
1		chopped scallion
2	cups	salted water
1	cup	dry vermouth
1		small green bell pepper, julienne for garnish
		shallot and red pepper sauce

PROCEDURE:

Using the saute method of cooking, prepare the lobster meat. Next make the panade. For the quenelles, put the lobster in a food processor and, using an "S" knife, run until smooth. Cut panade into small pieces, and add lobster one piece at a time. Add egg and remaining two egg yolks one at a time, and then add remaining 5 tbsp of butter, bit by bit. Blend in cayenne pepper, 1⁄2 tsp salt, and nutmeg. Transfer mixture to a bowl and stir in scallions. Chill until quite cold, almost freezing. Bring water and ver-mouth to a medium boil, form quenelles into cylinders with tapered ends, like small Cuban cigars, and slide into water. Poach until firm, 5–8 min. Remove from water, drain and transfer to a warm plate. Spoon red pepper sauce over warm quenelles and garnish with julienne green peppers. Serve immediately!

Note: Quenelles can be frozen and used at a later date so you can really make big batches of them if you wish.

Panade

Combine milk, cayenne pepper, 1/4 tsp salt, and 1 tbsp of the butter in a small saucepan. Cook over low heat just until butter melts. Add flour all at once. Cook over medium heat, stirring constantly until flour is cooked, all excess moisture evaporated, and a film coats the bottom of the pan (4–5 min). Remove from heat and cool slightly. Transfer to a food processor, add one egg yolk and whirl until smooth. Cover and chill 30 min.

Shallot/Red Pepper Sauce

3		large shallots, minced
1/4	cup	white wine vinegar
1/4	cup	dry white wine
2		red bell peppers
3		egg yolks
3/4	tsp	Dijon mustard
1/2	lb	melted butter

Put shallots, vinegar and wine into saucepan and reduce over medium heat to 2 tbsp. Set aside. In food processor, puree red peppers, add reduced shallot mixture, egg yolks and mustard and whirl until smooth. Add melted butter, and slowly add to the pepper puree.

LOBSTER MOUSSE

(4–6 servings)

This is great either as an appetizer or as an entree. Its color and texture make it not only tasty but attractive to the eye. You will need a food processor for this recipe. If you do not have one, a blender will do but is a little more work for the cook. I serve this a lot in the summer with various sauces on beds of beautifully colored lettuces and cabbages.

Note: This dish is done in three layers. That is why it is prepared in three separate steps. Don't be intimidated by the length of the instructions; it is really quite simple. Trust me!

INGREDIENTS:

6	oz	fresh shucked lobster meat
3	oz	fresh haddock
1	each	egg yolk
1	tsp	panade
1	pinch	saffron
1	pinch	salt
1/2	cup	all purpose cream

PROCEDURE:

Step 1 Reserve one whole claw of lobster meat per person for later. In a food processor using the knife attachment, place the haddock, cut up into 1 in. chunks. Then add the cooked lobster also cut up into small chunks. Turn on the machine and add lobster tomalley, egg yolk, saffron and salt. Run until very well chopped, about 2 min, and add the cream while still running. When mixed thoroughly, slowly add the panade. I usually break off little pieces and add it so that it mixes quickly. Don't let your panade get too stiff, or it will be hard to work with and won't combine well with the rest of the mousse mixture. It is best when it is soft and pliable. The final product should be very well pureed, sticky and mushy. If you have any lumps of any kind, run a little longer in the food processor. Place mixture into a well-greased 22 x 11 x 6 cm glass baking dish and set aside.

Step 2 Now for the duxelles, a hash of mushrooms, chopped shallots and herbs simmered in butter. The name derives from Uxel, a small town of the Cotes-du-Nord in northern France.

1.5	oz	clarified butter
1	cup	finely chopped mushrooms with stems
2	each	shallots finely chopped
1/8	tsp.	black pepper
1/4	tsp.	rubbed sage
1/4	tsp.	leaf thyme
1	pinch	nutmeg

In a 7 or 8 in. saute pan place the clarified butter and set on a high heat. When butter is hot, add the shallots and cook until shallots are evenly golden. Stir with a wooden spoon. Then add the finely chopped mushrooms and stems, again keep stirring. add the sage, thyme, black pepper, and nutmeg. Cook on a medium heat stirring constantly. Simmer for about 15 min, drain off any excess butter and set aside to cool. Cool for 10 min and place on top of the mixture you made in Step 1, evenly spread over the top.

Step 3 Almost the same as Step 1.

6	oz	boned and skinned salmon
1/2	cup	all purpose cream
1	each	egg yolk
1/4	tsp	black pepper
1/8	tsp	celery salt
1/8	tsp	garlic salt
1/2	tsp	panade

In the same food processor, using the same attachment, place the salmon cut into 1-in. chunks. Turn on food processor and start to puree, blend the cream and the egg yolk, and slowly add them to the salmon. Then add the pepper, salt and dill. Finally, add the panade in the same way you did in Step 1. Remove mixture and add to the glass baking dish on top of the duxelle. Spread mixture evenly over th top and then cover the baking dish with foil. Place the glass baking dish into a larger roasting pan and pour hot water into the roasting pan so that it comes up 1 in. on the side of the glass baking dish. Place in a preheated oven at 400°F. Bake for 45–50 min. Remove from oven, take foil off glass baking dish and cool.

To serve, take a sharp knife and run along the inside edge of the glass baking dish to loosen the mousse from the sides. Invert the dish onto a flat surface and the mousse will fall right out. If you are serving it as an entree, slice it lengthwise for a large dinner-sized piece and set it on bedded plate. If you are serving it as an appetizer, cut it across about 1 in. thick and and place it on a bedded appetizer plate. Top with the desired sauce, place the lobster claw on top of the sauce, and it is ready to serve.

This will last in the refrigerator for about three days, keep it covered at all times. It can also be frozen. If you freeze it, wrap it tightly in plastic film and then in freezer paper.

Note: The best way to serve this is on a colorful bed of lettuce or red cabbage. Top it with either a roasted red pepper sauce or an avocado cream sauce, or any sauce to your liking. The beds of lettuce I have used are red leaf lettuce, radicchio, green leaf lettuce, Boston lettuce, kale and my favorite red cabbage.

LOBSTER DUMPLINGS

(4 servings)

This is a chinese dish made with a won ton wrapping. It can either be steamed or deep fried. It makes a great little apppetizer at a cocktail party, and they are fun to make.

INGREDIENTS:

1	lb	cooked lobster lobster meat
1/4	tsp	finely chopped ginger root
1/2	tsp	Dijon mustard
1	ea	egg yolk, room temperature
1/2	cup	vegetable oil
8		wonton wrappers
		salt and pepper to taste
Egg wash		
1		egg, beaten
1/2	cup	water

PROCEDURE:

Finely chop the lobster meat and set aside. In a stainless steel bowl, whisk egg yolk and add oil 1 drop at a time until you have made a mayonnaise. Add the dijon mustard and the ginger root, salt and pepper to taste. Mix lobster meat and mayonaise together, lay won tons on counter and place lobster mixture in center of won ton. Wrap won ton around lobster mixture and seal with egg wash. Mix the beaten egg and the water to make an egg wash. If you steam these you might want to hold them shut with a tooth pick also. To steam bring water to a boil in a steamer place dumplings on steamer rack and and steam 5-7 minutes. To deep fry you can either steam them first and cool them or you can fry them directly after making them. If you were to steam them first, the won ton, like pasta, expands somewhat for a thicker skin consistency. If you go straight into the fry oil you will get a thin very crunchy crust altogether different. All three methods are very good and I suggest you try all three. To deep fry, place frying oil in a sauce pan about 1 in. deep. Heat to 350°F and place dumplings in hot oil. Fry on all sides until golden brown 3-5 min, remove from oil, pat dry of excess oil, and serve.

My favorite way to serve these little tidbits is on a bed of fresh purple kale with a chinese sweet and sour sauce, and chinese hot mustard. They are also good with a teriyaki glaze or bull dog sauce. All are available in your local super markets. Most supermarkets also carry won ton wrap in the produce section.

BAKED STUFFED ARTICHOKE HEARTS WITH LOBSTER

(4 servings)

INGREDIENTS:

6	each	artichoke hearts
1	1-lb	lobster, shucked, or 5 oz of meat *(optional)*
1	cup	lobster stuffing
1/2	cup	Hollandaise sauce

PROCEDURE:

Cut artichoke hearts in half and place in a ceramic baking dish. Slice the shucked lobster meat into bite-sized pieces and place over the artichoke hearts. Then cover with lobster stuffing and bake in a preheated oven at 400°F for 10 min. Remove from oven, top with Hollandaise sauce and serve.

LOBSTER TOAST

(20 slices)

This is a great accompaniment to lobster bisque or any other of my soups. My mother was a butter lover. A lot of the recipes she gave me called for a stick of butter (8 tablespoons).

INGREDIENTS:

1	stick	butter
10	oz	lobster meat, cooked
1	tbsp	lobster tomalley
2	tbsp	minced onion
2	tbsp	minced red pepper
1	tsp	chopped garlic
2	tbsp	chopped parsley
1	tbsp	grated parmesan
1	loaf	French bread
		cayenne pepper
		salt and pepper

PROCEDURE:

In a food processor place the lobster and tomalley and run until it turns into a mush. In a sauce pan add 1 tbsp of butter and add the onion, garlic, and red pepper; salt and pepper to taste and add a pinch of cayenne. Cook slowly until the vegetables are soft. In a medium-size bowl add the remaining butter, the mashed lobster and tomalley, the parsley, and the parmesan cheese. Blend thoroughly. Add the cooked vegetables and mix again. Slice the bread into 20 round slices. Preheat oven to 350°F and toast the bread rounds slightly on both sides. Remove from oven, spread with mixture of lobster butter, and return to oven for 5–7 min. Serve immediately.

♥♥♥♥

Sauces

AIOLI

(2 cups)

In France, aioli is known as "beurre de provence." It is basically a garlic mayonaise made with olive oil and lemon juice. The garlic flavor is very strong and dominant in this particular sauce.

INGREDIENTS:

4	each	garlic cloves, minced
2	each	egg yolks
1	cup	olive oil
1	each	lemon, squeezed
		salt and pepper

PROCEDURE:

Mince the garlic as finely as possible. In a mixing bowl add the garlic to the egg yolks and whip until frothy. Slowly pour in oil one drop at a time, whipping constantly. Squeeze all the juice from the lemon and add slowly. Salt and pepper to taste.

A variation of this sauce quite commonly used as an accompaniment in traditional Mediterranean soups can easily be made. If you add one tablespoon of crushed fresh hot chile pepper to the aioli, it becomes what the French call *rouille*.

BEARNAISE SAUCE

(1 cup)

INGREDIENTS:

2	each	shallots, minced
1/2	cup	white wine
4	tbsp	tarragon vinegar
3	tbsp	chopped tarragon
3	egg	yolks
1	cup	clarified butter
1	pinch	cayenne pepper

PROCEDURE:

Place shallots and wine in a saucepan with tarragon. Reduce over low heat until 3–4 tbsp of liquid is left. Strain off the excess liquid, leaving the tarragon reduction wet. In a double boiler, mix the egg yolks and slowly add the clarified butter, beating it in with a whisk. When the sauce is quite thick, remove it from heat. Add the tarragon reduction and cayenne pepper and mix well.

COCKTAIL SAUCE

There are many different recipes for cocktail sauce. This one is simple and very tangy—a little goes along way.

INGREDIENTS:

1	cup	chili sauce
1	tbsp	horseradish
1/4	tsp	black pepper
1/2	lemon	juice

PROCEDURE:

In a small bowl, mix all ingredients together. It is best to let stand 1 hr before serving. Serve very cold. This sauce also has a very long shelf life. Stored in a sealed container, it will last two weeks.

LOBSTER MAYONNAISE

INGREDIENTS:

1	cup	mayonnaise
2	cups	tomato concasse*
1	tbsp	lemon juice
1/4	cup	lobster fumet
1	cup	chopped basil

PROCEDURE:

In a bowl mix all the ingredients and refrigerate for one hour.

Tomato concasse is a French term for tomatoes that have been peeled, seeded and chopped. This is very easy to do. Simply put ripe tomatoes in hot boiling water for 10–12 sec. Remove and immediately place them in ice water. Peel off skin and discard. Then cut the tomato on its equator and squeeze out the seeds. Chop the tomato and place it in a colander to drain any excess liquid.

PESTO SAUCE

(6–8 servings)

INGREDIENTS:

2	cups	washed fresh basil leaves
4		large garlic cloves, minced
1	cup	shelled pistachios
1	cup	virgin olive oil
1	tbsp	fresh squeezed lemon juice
1	tsp	black pepper
3/4	cup	freshly grated parmesan cheese
1/4	cup	plain bread crumbs

PROCEDURE:

In a food processor bowl with a knife attachment, put basil leaves and chop for about 15 sec. Add garlic and pistachios and chop again until pistachios are finely chopped. Keep motor running and slowly add olive oil. Turn off machine and add remaining ingredients. Turn motor on for about 10 sec to blend thoroughly. Scrape out bowl into a container, cover and refrigerate until ready to use.

Note: This sauce is great warm or cold and will last at least a week under refrigeration. I keep plenty on hand all summer; it is one of my favorites.

REMOULADE SAUCE

(4 servings)

This is a mayonnaise-based sauce that is terrific with chilled shellfish, especially lobster.

INGREDIENTS:

1	cup	mayonnaise
1/4	cup	chopped parsley
1/4	cup	chopped capers
2		chopped anchovies
1/4	cup	chopped onion
1		garlic clove, finely chopped
1	tsp	Dijon mustard
1	tsp	fresh squeezed lemon juice

PROCEDURE:

In a bowl combine the mayonnaise with all the other ingredients and refrigerate for 1 hr before serving. This is like a very fancy tartar sauce and will last about three weeks in a sealed container, if kept refrigerated.

CREAMED LOBSTER SAUCE

(3 cups)

This is a great sauce to top any poached fish. It can used on any kind of seafood however it is cooked, but poached is my personal favorite.

INGREDIENTS:

1	lb	freshly shucked lobster meat, chopped
1/3	cup	butter or margarine
1/3	cup	all purpose flour
3	cups	milk
1	tbsp	Dijon mustard
1/8	tsp	black pepper
3	each	egg yolks
1/4	cup	cooking sherry
1	tbsp	brandy

PROCEDURE:

In a medium-size sauce pan bring milk to a scalding temperature, 180°F. In a 4-qt saucepan, melt butter. Using a wire whip, add flour and stir until smooth. Slowly add the hot milk, stirring constantly, until thick and smooth. Then add mustard and blend thoroughly. Simmer for about 5 min. Add egg yolks one at a time, and mix thoroughly. Add sherry, brandy and the lobster meat. Mix thoroughly again and serve.

TOMATO LOBSTER SAUCE

(3 cups)

INGREDIENTS:

1	tbsp	butter
2		finely chopped shallots
1	tbsp	flour
1	cup	milk
1/4	cup	tomato paste
1	tsp	dijon mustard
1	lb	cooked lobster meat, chopped
3	tbsp	cooking sherry
1/2	cup	heavy cream
1/2	tsp	white wine worcestershire
1	dash	tobasco

PROCEDURE:

In a medium-sized saute pan, melt the butter on a medium high heat and add the shallots. Cook until they just start to brown. Stir in the flour, milk, tomato paste and mustard, and bring to a boil. Using a wire whisk, stir constantly. Reduce to a simmer add the lobster, sherry, cream, worcestershire and tobasco. Mix thoroughly and cook until sauce begins to bubble. Remove from heat and serve.

HOLLANDAISE SAUCE

(2 cups)

INGREDIENTS:

6	each	egg yolks
1.5	cups	clarified butter
1	tbsp	fresh squeezed lemon juice
1	tsp	white wine vinegar
		cayenne pepper

PROCEDURE:

To clarify butter, place unsalted butter in saucepan and heat at medium-low. As the butter melts, the fats and solids will rise to the top. Skim the fats off with a ladle until you are left with a clear butter. In a medium-sized stainless-steel bowl, place the egg yolks, lemon juice and vinegar. Whisk with a wire whip until frothy. Heat at medium-low until egg mixture is warm. Whisk constantly as you slowly add the butter, using a small ladle. If the eggs get too hot remove from heat and continue to add butter. If sauce becomes too thick, add a little room-temperature water until smooth. The formula for a safe Hollandaise sauce is two ounces of butter for every egg yolk. Add cayenne pepper to taste.

GREEN PEPPERCORN SAUCE

(1 cup)

INGREDIENTS:

1	tbsp	clarified butter
1	oz	brandy
2	tbsp	green peppercorns
1/4	cup	lobster fumet
1	pint	all-purpose cream

PROCEDURE:

In a shallow saucepan, heat clarified butter over medium high heat. Add peppercorns. When they start to pop, add brandy and flame. Pour in lobster fumet, bring to a boil and add cream. Reduce liquid to half and serve.

LOBSTER BEURRE BLANC SAUCE

(2 cups

INGREDIENTS:

1/4	cup	red wine vinegar
1/4	cup	white wine
1/4	cup	lobster stock
2		large shallots, minced
3	cups	whipped unsalted butter, room temperature
1/2	tsp	cracked black pepper
		salt to taste

PROCEDURE:

In a small sauce pan, place shallots, vinegar, wine and lobster stock. Over high heat reduce liquid to 3 tbsp. Remove from heat and let stand for 2 min. One tablespoon at a time, slowly whisk into the liquid the whipped butter until sauce is light and fluffy. Whisk in black pepper and serve immediately.

Note: Lobster beurre blanc is my favorite but you can try a variety of sauces: hollandaise, bearnaise, newburg or mornay.

WHITE SAUCE, CREAM SAUCE, BECHAMEL

(4 cups)

INGREDIENTS:

1	qt	milk
1/2	lb	margarine or butter
1	cup	flour
1	tsp	white wine worcestershire
1	tbsp	dijon mustard
1/2	cup	lobster fumet or lobster stock *(optional)*

PROCEDURE:

In a 2-qt double boiler, bring 1 qt of milk to 180°F. While the milk is heating, melt the margarine in a small saucepan. When the margarine is totally melted, add the flour. With a wire whip mix thoroughly. Slowly add the roux to the scalded milk and stir constantly with the wire whip. Sauce will thicken. Keep whipping to avoid lumping. Add the dijon mustard, mix thoroughly and then add the lobster fumet. Slowly whip until smooth. That's it.

CREAM OF LOBSTER AND SHALLOT SAUCE

(2 cups)

This is a great sauce for poached white fish like pollock, cod, haddock and sole.

INGREDIENTS:

1	oz	pureed body and leg meat
1	tbsp	lobster tomalley *(optional)*
8	oz	dry white wine
2	oz	lemon juice
2	tbsp	lobster stock
4	oz	heavy cream
4	oz	butter cut into 1/2" cubes
4	tb	shallots, chopped
		salt and pepper

PROCEDURE:

In a saucepan, cook the shallots, white wine, lobster stock and lemon juice until all but 1 tbsp of the liquid has evaporated. Add the cream and bring to a strong boil, whisking constantly. Add the lobster meat and whip in the small pieces of butter until melted. Remove from heat. Season to taste with salt and pepper. Use as a top sauce or a pooled sauce for your prepared seafood.

Salads

LOBSTER AND ROTINI SALAD WITH TOMATO VINAIGRETTE

(4 servings)

Fresh herbs and freshly shucked lobster make this a beautiful dish. It is one of my favorite summer dishes. Add a nice cold bottle of white wine and some crisp French bread and I'm in heaven.

INGREDIENTS:

1	lb	freshly shucked lobster meat
1.5	cups	tomato vinaigrette
3	cups	cooked spinach rotini, chilled

Tomato Vinaigrette

1/4	cup	red wine vinegar
1	tsp	balsamic vinegar
1/4	cup	fresh mixed herbs (basil, tarragon, thyme, fennel, oregano, dill)
1	tbsp	minced shallots
1	tbsp	minced garlic
1	tsp	coarsely ground black pepper
1	cup	virgin olive oil

PROCEDURE:

Prepare one cup of tomato *concasse*—a French term for tomatoes that have been peeled, seeded and chopped. Put ripe tomatoes in hot boiling water for 10–12 sec. Remove and immediately place in ice water. Peel off skin and discard. Then cut the tomato on its equator and squeeze out the seeds. Chop the tomato and place in a colander to drain any excess liquid and place in a bowl. Add the above ingredients. Toss briefly. On four seperate chilled salad plates, first place rotini and then place chunks of the lobster meat on top of the rotini. Top with tomato vinaigrette and serve.

Note: This does not taste very good using dried herbs, so use only fresh herbs.

CURRIED LOBSTER SALAD

(2–4 servings)

INGREDIENTS:

2	1–2 lb	lobsters cooked and shucked
1/4	cup	minced onion
1/4	cup	minced celery
1	tsp	Dijon mustard
1/4	tsp	leaf thyme
2	dashes	white wine Worcestershire sauce
1/4	tsp	curry powder
1/8	tsp	black pepper
1/4	tsp	salt
4	tbsp	mayonaise
1	tsp	chopped parsley

PROCEDURE:

Cut the shucked lobster meat into bite-sized pieces and set aside. Place lobster tomalley and roe, if any, in a small bowl to add later. In a medium-sized bowl, combine all other ingredients, then add lobster meat and tomalley. Mix thoroughly and serve.

CLASSIC LOBSTER SALAD

(2–4 servings)

This is my basic lobster salad recipe. It is great to serve in a variety of different ways.

INGREDIENTS:

2	1–2 lb	lobsters cooked and shucked
1/4	cup	minced onion
1/4	cup	minced celery
1	tsp	Dijon mustard
1/4	tsp	leaf thyme
2	dashes	white wine Worcestershire sauce
1/8	tsp	black pepper
1/4	tsp	salt
4	tbsp	mayonaise
1	tsp	chopped parsley

PROCEDURE:

Cut the shucked lobster meat into bite-sized pieces and set aside. Place lobster tomalley and roe, if any, in a small bowl to add later. In a medium-sized bowl combine all other ingredients, then add lobster meat and tomalley, mix thoroughly and serve.

LOBSTER SALAD ROLL

(2 servings)

This is a classic Maine luncheon. From Kittery to Eastport you'll find the lobster roll on almost every luncheon menu. They are easy to make, and anybody who loves lobster will love a good lobster roll.

INGREDIENTS:

2		hot dog rolls
1	tsp	softened butter or margarine
1/2	cup	shredded lettuce
1.5	cups	lobster salad

PROCEDURE:

Butter both sides of the hot dog rolls with the butter or margarine. Place in a skillet over medium heat and cook until golden brown on both sides. Place shredded lettuce in bottom of roll, then add the lobster salad. Sprinkle with paprika and serve. One of my favorite ways to serve this is with homemade potato chips and a really crisp half of a sour pickle.

STUFFED TOMATO WITH LOBSTER SALAD

(4 servings)

INGREDIENTS:

2 or 4		large tomatoes
1–2	cups	lobster salad
4–8	leaves	Bibb lettuce

PROCEDURE:

Arrange Bibb lettuce on chilled salad plate. Using a sharp knife cut the tomato from the top almost all the way through into eight equal segments. Cut in half first then into quarters, etc. Spread segments out to leave room for lobster salad in the middle. Put the tomato in the center of the lettuce, fill with salad and sprinkle with paprika, garnish with fresh fruit and vegetables, and serve.

There are many variations to this. Simply by changing the vegetable you can make a lot of different stuffed salads. Try these:

Cucumber boats: Peel and hollow out seeds from a cucumber and slice it lengthwise to make two equal boats. Place on lettuce and stuff with lobster salad.

Zuchini and summer squash boats: Follow recipe for cucumber but do not peel the skin.

Stuffed peppers: With the wide variety of bell peppers on the market today you can really make colorful presentations. Bell peppers are now available in supermarkets in the following colors, green, red, yellow, orange and blue. These peppers look especially beautiful filled with lobster salad and topped with alfalfa sprouts.

LOBSTER CAESAR SALAD

(4 servings)

INGREDIENTS:

3	each	anchovy
3	tbsp	olive oil
1	tsp	chopped garlic
2	tsp	red wine vinegar
2	tsp	Dijon mustard
5	dash	Worcestershire sauce
1	each	coddled egg yolk
1/2	each	squeezed lemon
1/4	cup	parmesan cheese
1/2	head	romaine lettuce, torn not cut
1/2	cup	croutons
1/4	tsp	freshly ground black pepper
4	each	lobster claws

PROCEDURE:

In a medium-size wooden salad bowl, mash the anchovies and the garlic with a fork and rub the inside of the bowl with it. Then add the vinegar and mustard, blend thoroughly. Using the fork add the olive oil and the egg yolk (*note:* the term coddled means to cook in simmering water for 1 min), mix together and add the Worcestershire, lemon, and parmesan cheese. Add the romaine lettuce and the croutons, and then toss salad until all the lettuce is coated with the dressing. Using salad forks portion the salad into edible cheese baskets, add a lobster claw to each and serve immediately.

Edible Cheese Basket

1 1/3 cups	Kraft 100% grated parmesan cheese

On high heat place an 8" non-stick sauté pan and heat for about 1 min. Place the grated cheese in the pan and turn the pan so that the cheese covers the inside of the pan. Cook for 1 min, remove from heat, invert the pan, and tap the pan on a counter right on top of an upside down cereal bowl. Repeat this procedure until all baskets are made. Let the baskets cool on the cereal bowls for at least 2 min before handling. Gently take baskets off the cereal bowls, Turn right side up and place on salad plate.

Brunch

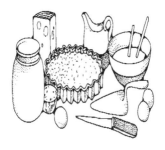

EGGS DE BOUCHARD

(4 servings)

Eggs de Bouchard is a variation of Eggs Benedict. It is fresh shucked lobster, sauteed in butter and placed on English muffins or crumpets, topped with poached eggs and covered with Bearnaise sauce.

INGREDIENTS:

1	tsp	butter
4		English muffins or crumpets, split
8		eggs
2		1-lb lobsters, cooked and shucked
2	cups	Bearnaise sauce (see *Sauces*)
1	tbsp	white vinegar
2	qts	water, for poaching
		salt and pepper

PROCEDURE:

Slice tails and claws of lobster meat lengthwise. In a large shallow pan, bring to a boil water and vinegar. Toast English muffins and set on plate. Lightly saute lobster until warm. Be careful not to overcook, or lobster will become tough. Arrange lobster meat on top of all English muffins evenly. Drop eggs in water and poach until white is cooked but yolk is still runny. Remove from water with slotted spatula, drain completely and place on top of lobster meat. Top egg with Bearnaise sauce and serve.

LOBSTER RAREBIT

(4 servings)

INGREDIENTS:

1	qt	milk
1/2	lb	margarine or butter
1	cup	flour
1	tsp	white wine worcestershire
1	tbsp	Dijon mustard
1/2	cup	lobster fumet or lobster stock *(optional)*
2		egg yolks
2	cups	grated extra-sharp white cheddar cheese
1	cup	dark beer or ale
1	tbsp	paprika
1	tsp	dry mustard
1	tbsp	Worcestershire sauce
1	lb	freshly shucked lobster meat
8	slices	whole wheat bread, toasted
		cayenne pepper

PROCEDURE:

In a 2-qt double boiler, bring 1 qt of milk to 180°F. While the milk is heating, in a small sauce pan melt the margarine. When the margarine is totally melted add the flour, and mix thoroughly with a wire whip. Slowly add the roux to the scalded milk, stirring constantly with the whip. This makes a roux. The sauce will thicken; keep whipping to avoid lumping. Add the Dijon mustard mix and then the lobster fumet, slowly, and then add the cheddar cheese. Using a wire whisk, completely blend the cheese. In a separate bowl mix ale, mustard, Worcestershire and paprika. Add to double boiler slowly so that sauce does not thin too much. It should be relatively thick. Cut the toast into quarters. In indivdual baking dishes or boats place place 8 toast points and 4 oz of lobster each. Top with 1 cup of rarebit sauce and bake at 350°F for 5–7 min. Remove from heat and serve immediately.

LOBSTER QUICHE

(4–6 servings)

Whenever I put this on a lunch or brunch menu it is always the first to get swooped up. It's a hit no matter when you serve it.

INGREDIENTS:

1	each	pie shell
6	each	eggs, well beaten
1.5	cups	sour cream
1/2	tsp	Worcestershire sauce
1/4	tsp	black pepper
1	tsp	Dijon mustard
1	cup	grated swiss cheese
1	cup	grated sharp cheddar cheese
1/2	cup	chopped scallions
6	oz	lobster meat, chopped

PROCEDURE:

Preheat your oven to 375°F. In a medium-sized mixing bowl blend together the eggs, sour cream, Worcestershire, pepper and Dijon mustard. (This mixture is the quiche batter.) Arrange your pie dough in a pie shell. In another bowl toss the two cheeses with the scallions and lobster. Then place the lobster mixture into the pie shell. Add the quiche batter, sprinkle with paprika, and place in oven. Cook for 45 min or until top of quiche is golden brown. Remove from heat and let stand for 15 min, then serve.

Note: This can also be made ahead of time and then reheated. It comes out excellently if you microwave each piece for 2 min on full power. If you are reheating in a conventional oven set oven at 425°F and heat for 10–12 min.

LOBSTER BENEDICT

(4 servings)

This is a great brunch item and a variation of the classic dish Eggs Benedict. It is quite simple to make and very delicious to eat.

INGREDIENTS:

2	1 lb	lobsters cooked and shucked
8	ea	large eggs
4	ea	English muffins, split
2	cups	Hollandaise sauce
2	qts	water
1	tsp	white wine vinegar

PROCEDURE:

Slice tails and claws of lobster meat lengthwise. In a large, shallow pan bring water and vinegar to a boil. Toast English muffins and set on plate. Arrange lobster meat on top of all English muffins evenly. Drop eggs in water and poach until white is cooked but yolk is still runny. Remove from water with slotted spatula, drain completely, and place eggs on top of lobster meat. Top with Hollandaise sauce and serve.

AVOCADO AND LOBSTER LOUIS

(4 servings)

An avocado filled with fresh shucked lobster meat topped with Louis dressing, topped with caviar and garnished with fresh fruit. This makes an ideal summer brunch or lunch dish. The contrast between the bright colors of the fruit and the red cabbage is simply beautiful.

INGREDIENTS:

4	ea	ripe avocados, skinned and pit discarded
4	1-lb	lobsters cooked and shucke
		(about 1 lbof meat)
1	head	red cabbage
1	lb	green grapes
1	pint	fresh strawberries, hulled
2	ea	oranges, peeled and sliced
2	ea	apples cut into wedges
1.5	cups	Louis sauce
1/2	oz	caviar *(optional)*

PROCEDURE:

On individual chilled plates place a bed of red cabbage. In the center place avocados on top of cabbage. Fill avocado with chucks of lobster meat. Arrange fresh fruit around avocados. Cover lobster with Louis sauce, sprinkle caviar over sauce, and serve.

Louis sauce

1.5	cups	mayonaise
1/4	cup	chopped capers
1	tsp	dijon mustard
1/4	cup	red pepper relish
1/3	cup	chili sauce
1/4	tsp	onion powder
1/4	tsp	black pepper
1	tbsp	lemon juice

In a bowl blend all ingredients and chill for one hour.

LOBSTER FRITTATA

(4 servings)

Preparation time, 20 minutes. A frittata, simply put, is an open-faced omelet. You can be as creative as you want with the ingredients you put on one. They are also very easy to make. A frittata can be served either as a brunch item or for breakfast.

INGREDIENTS:

6	oz	lobster meat
5	ea	whole eggs, well beaten
5	ea	egg whites, well beaten
3	tsp	olive oil
1	tbsp	chopped fresh herbs: basil, tarragon and thyme
3/4	cup	shredded mozzarella cheese
2	ea	large plum tomatoes, sliced
1/2	ea	red pepper, cut into julienne strips
2	ea	scallions, sliced into quarter-inch rounds
2	tbsp	sliced black olives
1	tsp	chopped parsley

optional garnishes: radish flowers, fresh dill, cherry tomatoes

PROCEDURE:

In a small mixing bowl, combine the whole eggs and the egg whites, and using a wire whip, beat vigorously. Add the mozzarella cheese and the fresh chopped herbs to the egg mixture. In a small-size skillet or sauté pan place 1 teaspoon of olive oil, and add the tomatoes, scallions, red peppers, black olives and lobster meat. On medium high heat, sauté these ingredients until tomatoes loose their firmness but not their shape, and set aside. In a medium-size (nonstick 10-inch) skillet or sauté pan, add the remaining olive oil and place pan over high heat. When oil is hot, add egg mixture, reduce heat to medium, and cook the frittata until nearly firm.

With a rubber spatula, lift the edges to let the undercooked egg run underneath, about 6 minutes. If you are an experienced omelet maker, you can flip the omelet at this time and cook it on both sides, although this is not necessary.

At this point place the lobster and vegetable mix on top of the frittata, in the following order—arrange tomatoes first, then arrange red peppers, lobster, black olives and scallions. Cook over low heat 1 more minute, remove from heat, salt and pepper to taste, cut into wedges, and serve. Garnish with radish flowers, fresh dill and chopped parsley. Bon Appetit!

CHICKEN AND LOBSTER ROULADE

(4 servings)

This roulade is chicken, stuffed with lobster, rolled and tied in cheesecloth and poached in a *court bouillon* (water for poaching flavored with different ingredients.) This dish is low in fat and can be prepared two days in advance. It is always served chilled and makes a great brunch or lunch item. I serve it with pickled asparagus and potato salad because they complement the dish well.

INGREDIENTS:

4	ea	boneless, skinless chicken breasts (6 oz)
4	oz	lobster meat
2	tbsp	mayonnaise
1	cup	roasted red pepper puree

PROCEDURE:

First make your court bouillon (see next page). Then clean the chicken breasts free of any fat, then lay the breasts on a flat surface with the inside of the breast facing up. Smear the inside of the breast with a thin layer of mayonnaise, then add the ounce of lobster to each breast.

Roll the breasts so they look like small logs. Then wrap each breast in cheesecloth and tie them with twine by starting at one end of the log and spiralling the twine around the cloth, keeping the meat tight.

Poach the breasts in the bouillon for 12 min, then remove and chill for at least 2 hr. Remove cheesecloth after they are completely chilled and slice the breast on a diagonal. Place sauce on plate and layer the pieces over the sauce, garnish and serve!

Court Bouillon

2	qts	water
1⁄4	cup	carrots, cut
1⁄4	cup	celery, cut
1	ea	shallot
4	ea	bay leaves
1	cup	white wine
1	tsp	salt
6	ea	black peppercorns
1	sprig	thyme

Make the court bouillon by placing all the ingredients for the bouillon in a 3- or 4-quart pot and bring it to a medium boil.

Tomalley

When I was a child we had a summer house in Marshfield, Massachusetts. Because we lived right on the ocean we got a lot of company, and I loved it when we'd have a lobster bake. My mother always boiled her lobsters and we'd all sit down to eat them. A lot of times we'd have to explain to our guests how to eat lobsters. I would tell them about the tomalley, the grayish green stuff in the body of the lobster shell. Most of the friends and relatives that visited would not touch it. The thought of eating it was out of the question, YUK! When everyone was done my mother and I would clear the table and take all the lobster bodies back to the kitchen. We'd quickly scoop out all the tomalley and put it in a bowl for later.

I love tomalley on toast in the morning, tomalley scrambled eggs, and tomalley stuffed mushrooms. My mother used to freeze it. Whenever we had a party the tomalley was thawed, and all sorts of things—spreads and dips, baked mushrooms and great little party canapes—were whipped together for many of the same people who wouldn't touch the stuff in the body shell. We never let on that we used it in the things we made, but we often we used tomalley in anything we wanted to taste like lobster.

Tomalley is actually the lobster's liver. It is a digestive gland that forms blood plasma by metabolizing the food the lobster eats. The old theory that lobsters are scavengers, eating mainly dead things, is not 100 percent true. Scientists have studied the lobster's digestive system and found fresh food in their stomachs. They eat crabs, mussels, clams, sea urchins, starfish and even other lobsters. Many useful nutrients like proteins, vitamins and minerals are extracted by the lobster's liver, making it very good to eat. Because it is an organ, its flavor is much stronger that that of the muscle tissue found in the lobster's claws and tail. I have enjoyed it all my life and if you're a lobster lover you'll love all the great things you can do with the tomalley.

When I was the chef at Whitneys' Inn in Jackson, New Hampshire, we had a lobster bake every Wednesday night. Sometimes we cooked as many as 100 lobsters for the guests. I really wanted to take all the lobster bodies back to the kitchen when they were done, because I could see all that beautiful tomalley going to waste. I even asked Terry (the owner) if we could save the lobster bodies before they hit the trash barrels, but to no avail—they were always "deep-sixed." The Innkeepers thought I was nuts, but I knew all the great things I could create with that tomalley.

You can buy lobster tomalley. Most fish stores that sell lobsters have to check their tanks each morning to see if any lobsters died overnight, or if any are so weak and limp that they are about to die. These lobsters are called "sleepers." They are immediately cooked. The tomalley and coral are scooped out and put in half-pint containers. You can even request that they do this for you. Some will sell you the lobster bodies with the tomalley intact. This is the best way to get it if you can, because you get the body as well. The bodies can be chopped or crushed so you can make up stocks and fumets. I use every part of the lobster I can, not just the meat.

Don't throw away your lobster bodies, and the next time you're in the fish store ask if they have any cooked lobster bodies for sale. They're usually about ten cents apiece. If they don't have any then ask them to save them for you.

TOMALLEY ON TOAST

Toast your favorite kind of bread and, while it's hot, butter it with room-temperature butter. Then spread tomalley on top of the butter, the thicker the better. If you have any of the roe put that on too.

TOMALLEY BUTTER

Great on grilled fish. Place one stick of softened, salted butter into a mixing bowl and whip with an electric beater until smooth and fluffy. Add 1/4 tsp of black pepper and 1/4 cup of lobster tomalley to the butter, and whip again.

TOMALLEY
SCRAMBLED EGGS

(2 servings)

INGREDIENTS:

1	tbsp	clarified butter
5	each	eggs, beaten
1/4	cup	tomalley butter, softened
2	tbsp	sour cream

PROCEDURE:

In a small skillet heat butter over moderate heat. While butter is heating, blend together eggs, tomalley butter and sour cream. Pour mixture into pan and stir with a wooden fork until light and fluffy. Serve immediately.

TOMALLEY SPREAD

(2 cups)

Great with crackers or raw vegetables.

INGREDIENTS:

1.5	cups	cream cheese
1/4	cup	sour cream
1	tsp	Dijon mustard
1	tbsp	fresh chopped chives
1/4	tsp	Worcestershire sauce
1/2	cup	tomalley
1/4	tsp	lemon juice
1/2	tsp	lemon zests
1	pinch	cayenne pepper

PROCEDURE:

Place all ingredients in a mixing bowl and beat with an electric hand beater until smooth and creamy.

TOMALLEY DIP

(2 cups)

Great with homemade potato chips.

INGREDIENTS:

1.5	cups	sour cream
1/2	cup	lobster tomalley
1	4-oz	can chopped clams *(optional)*

PROCEDURE:

Mix and serve.

TOMALLEY STUFFING

(2 cups)

INGREDIENTS:

2	cups	crushed Ritz crackers
1/2	cup	lobster
1/4	cup	melted butter
1	tbsp	sherry
1	tbsp	grated parmesan cheese
1	tsp	black pepper

PROCEDURE:

Mix all ingredients in bowl and refrigerate for 1/2 hr.

TOMALLEY MUSHROOMS

Parboil for about 2 min as many large mushrooms caps as you want to serve. Remove from water, drain and pat dry on paper towels. Stuff caps with tomalley stuffing and place on sheet pan. Put pan in preheated oven at 400°F for 12–15 min. Serve immediately.

TOMALLEY TOMATOES

Cut in half as many tomatoes as you wish to serve. Hollow out center enough to hold about 1/4 in. of stuffing. Place about 2 tbsps of tomalley stuffing on top of each tomato half. Put tomatoes on baking sheet and place in preheated oven at 400°F for 10–12 min. Serve immediately.

SCALLOPS WITH TOMALLEY

(4 servings)

INGREDIENTS:

2	lbs	sea scallops
2	cups	tomalley stuffing
1	cup	clarified butter

PROCEDURE:

Lay the scallops in a large shallow baking dish. Cover them with tomalley stuffing and drizzle butter over entire dish. Place dish in preheated oven at 350°F and cook for 30–35 min or until stuffing is golden brown. Portion onto dinner plates and serve.

LOBSTER TOMALLEY PATE

I love this recipe because it makes me feel like I am standing right beside an ocean wave. The smell and taste of the sea is right there. It's easy to make and a real hit at a cocktail party.

INGREDIENTS:

1	cup	lobster tomalley, and coral (if any)
5	oz	raw salmon flesh
3	oz	raw white fish (cod, haddock, pollack, etc.)
1/4	tsp	black pepper
1/4	tsp	paprika
1/4	tsp	celery salt
1/4	tsp	Old Bay seasoning
1/4	tsp	curry powder
3	threads	saffron
2	cups	whipped butter

PROCEDURE:

Finely chop all the raw fish and place in a bowl for mixing. Add all the spices and the cooked lobster tomalley and coral, and blend thoroughly. Place mixture in a shallow baking dish and bake at 400°F for 15 min. Remove from baking dish and place hot mixture into food processor. Run motor for 1 min to puree the mixture. Place in glass bowl and chill for 2 hr. Remove mixture from cold container and, in a large mixing bowl, blend together with the whipped butter. Whipped butter should be at room temperature, 70°F. When completely blended, place mixture in small pate mold or bread pan and chill for 1/2 hr. Remove pate from mold and place on a platter covered with red cabbage. Garnish with chopped egg white, chopped egg yolk, capers, whole grain mustard and chopped red onions. Serve with crisp French bread or crackers.

LOBSTER TOMALLEY SAUSAGE

(4 servings)

This is a really fun recipe to make, with a very rewarding final product. The first time I made lobster sausage I felt like a German scientist working on an experiment that would change the world. I had more ingredients on my eight-food work table than I knew what to do with. I enjoyed creating the sausages but I dreaded cleaning up the mess. When I was young I used to pay my younger sisters a quarter to clean up my mess, but they've all grown up now and moved away. I thought I'd try the same strategy on my daughter. She said she'd help me clean up if I bought her the "Teenage Mutant Ninja Turtle" movie. I thought about it and ended up cleaning up the mess myself. Have fun!

INGREDIENTS:

3⁄4	cup	chopped sea scallops
1⁄4	cup	chopped scallions
1	tbsp	fresh squeezed lime juice
1	tsp	black pepper
1	dash	Worcestershire sauce
1⁄8	tsp	celery salt
6	oz	cooked salmon, coarsely chopped
2	tsp	sugar
1	tbsp	salted butter, softened
1	tbsp	minced shallots
1	oz	brandy
1⁄2	cup	cooked lentils, patted dry
6	oz	raw lobster meat, chopped and squeezed dry
1	tsp	paprika
1⁄2	tsp	dry mustard
1⁄4	tsp	garlic salt

PROCEDURE:

You will need a pastry bag with a very wide plain tube and some string to make your sausages. Casings may be purchased at your local butcher shop, a butcher supply shop, or specialty store. Rinse casings in cold running water and then soak them in aciduated water. Allow them to dry before you fill them.

In a small bowl place the scallops, scallions, lime juice, black pepper, Worcestershire and Tabasco. Let stand for 20 min. While scallops are marinating take another bowl and add the celery salt, salmon, sugar, butter and shallots, and mix thoroughly. It is best if the salmon is a little warm (90–100°F); it makes the butter and shallots blend together better. Then add the brandy, lentils, lobster, tomalley, paprika, dry mustard and garlic salt. Mix thoroughly. Drain scallop mixture through a chinois and press on the solids to get out as much juice as possible. Add scallop mixture to the rest of the ingredients and blend. Lightly beat egg whites and add to the mixture. Chill mixture for one half hour.

Place the mixture in a pastry bag. Tie one end of each casing securely. Then one at a time fit the open end of the casing over the nozzle of the pastry tube until you have reached the tied end of the casing. Squeeze the pastry bag, forcing the mixture into the casing. Do not fill too tight. When you have enough of the mixture in the casing to make a 3-in. sausage, twist the casing once and then tie with string. Repeat until all the mixture is gone.

Bring two quarts of court bouillon to a boil in a large shallow pan. Reduce heat so bouillon is at a simmer and add the sausages. Place another shallow pan over the sausages to keep them submerged. Simmer for 20–30 min. Carefully remove sausages from bouillon and allow to cool. Place sausages on a charcoal grill and grill lightly for 10–12 min. Make sure charcoals are not too hot. I prefer the coals cool enough so the casings just lightly brown and do not burn. Serve them with a variety of accompaniments like tomalley mayonaise, aioli, jalepeno chutney, remoulade sauce, green tomato relish or pommery mustard sauce.

GRILLED RADICCHIO, LOBSTER AND FENNEL SALAD

This is a very elegant salad that goes well with a cold glass of white wine and French bread. The key to this salad is using fennel that is as fresh as possible.

INGREDIENTS:

2	heads	radicchio
1/2	cup	olive oil
1.2	lbs	fresh shucked lobster meat
1.5	cups	fennel and tomalley vinaigrette
		salt and pepper

Fennel and Tomalley Vinaigrette

1/2	cup	fresh chopped fennel bulb
1/8	cup	Balsamic vinegar
1/4	cup	fresh squeezed lemon juice
1/4	cup	minced shallots
2	tbsp	lobster tomalley, cooked
1	tsp	sugar
1/4	tsp	fresh ground pepper, coarse
1	cup	extra virgin olive oil

PROCEDURE:

Put all vinaigrette ingredients in a bowl and mix thoroughly. Then start a charcoal fire and allow the coals to become completely white before grilling the radicchio.

While the coals are getting ready, cut the lobster into bite-sized pieces, place in a bowl and cover with the vinaigrette. Remove outer leaves of the radicchio until you get to the bright red leaves. Cut the heads through the cores into quarters. Seperate all the leaves and put them in a large bowl. Pour the olive oil over them and sprinkle with salt and pepper. Let stand for 15–20 min.

Grill each leaf of radicchio, being careful not to let them burn. Arrange the grilled radicchio onto salad plates, evenly distribute the lobster and fennel mixture on top of the radicchio and serve.

107

LOBSTER TOMALLEY MAYONNAISE

(1 cup)

Mayonnaise is one of the most commonly used sauces in the American household today. Most people, including myself, buy commercial mayonnaise, but every once in awhile it is nice to savor a homemade mayonnaise. The next time you prepare a seafood dish that calls for mayonnaise try this particular recipe. You'll be delightfully surprised at how much it adds to the total flavor of the dish.

INGREDIENTS:

1	each	egg yolk
1	tsp	salt
1/2	tsp	dry mustard
1/4	tsp	freshly ground white pepper
1	tbsp	fresh squeezed lemon juice
1	cup	olive oil
2	tbsp	lobster tomalley

PROCEDURE:

Using a rotary beater and a stainless steel bowl, drop egg yolk into bowl. Add spices and lemon juice and beat on high until mixture is a frothy pale yellow. Add the oil ever so slowly, almost one drop at a time, beating constantly. If you add oil too fast the mayonnaise will curdle. If the mayonnaise gets too thick, add a little more lemon juice or water. When all the oil is added, add the tomalley. Refrigerate for 1 hr before serving.

Entrees

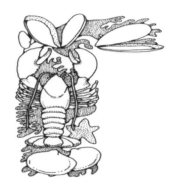

WALKER'S POINT LOBSTER

(4 servings)

Until last year only a handful of people outside the state of Maine knew where Walker's Point was. With all the publicity it receives now, it is hard to find anyone who does not know that it is the summer home of President George Bush. Knowing how much the President loves the state of Maine and in particular the town of Kennebunkport, I created this dish and named it after his summer home. I sent him a copy of the recipe for him and his family to enjoy. I hope you like it too.

This is truly a beautiful dish—fresh shucked lobster meat served on a bed of sauteed radicchio and chopped hazelnuts, topped with a beurre blanc sauce, pureed blueberries, and garnished with caviar. The presentation is subtle and at the same time magnificent. The red radicchio, the white beurre blanc sauce and puree of blueberries is more than symbolic, it is a pleasure to the eyes.

INGREDIENTS:

4		1–2 lb lobsters
1	head	radicchio, thinly sliced
1	tbsp	clarified butter
1/8	tsp	black pepper
1/4	cup	chopped hazelnuts (wild if possible)
1	cup	beurre blanc sauce
1/2	cup	blueberries
1	tsp	sugar
1	oz	caviar *(optional)*

PROCEDURE:

The assembly of this dish is key to its success. In preparing the lobster use the boiled method, with a slight variation. Prior to cooking flatten the tail of the lobster on a countertop. Turn the lobster on its back and place a skewer lengthwise between the swimmer-ets, until the tip of the skewer is at the bottom of the body. Using butcher's twine secure the skewer to the tail by wrapping the twine around both the shell of the tail and the skewer. The purpose of this is to keep the lobster tail from curling. When the lobster is cooked remove from water and cool. When you remove the skewer the tail will stay extended.

The key to the presentation of this dish is to reassemble the cooked lobster meat on the bed of radicchio in its original shape. So carefully shuck the meat from the shell. Dislocate the large claws from the the body and remove. Using a pair of heavy-duty cooking shears cut the knuckle shell and claw shell on both sides, being careful to keep the meat intact. Using the same proce-dure cut the tail shell carefully from the tail meat, keeping the tail attached to the body of the lobster. Set the lobster parts aside.

In a small saucepan, place blueberries and sugar and cook over medium heat until blueberries are soft and mushy, about 15 min. Remove from heat and, using either a blender or food processor, puree the blueber-ries. Set them aside at room temperature or in a warm bath of water (see note).

Next make the beurre blanc (see *Sauces*). Take one half cup of the beurre blanc and add to it the pureed blueberries, and keep warm, 80-90 deg.

In a medium-sized saute pan heat the clarified butter on medium high heat. Add the thinly sliced radicchio and saute for 1-2 min, just enough to get the radicchio hot, but do not let it loose its bright color. Remove from heat and arrange on a plate in a strip about 3 in. wide and the full diameter of the plate. I find an oval plate to work best. This is the bed on which you will place the lobster. Set the body shell of the lobster on the plate so that the bottom of the shell is at the center of the plate. Anatomically reassemble the shucked lobster body parts so that the lobster looks intact and whole again. Take one half cup of the beurre blanc sauce and mix it with the pureed blueberries and set to the side. Top the lobster with the beurre blanc sauce and then zig zag the blue beurre blanc sauce over the white beurre blanc and finish with chopped hazelnuts. Serve immediately.

Note: Mixing the blueberries and the beurre blanc can cause some difficulty if they are not the same temperature, so be sure to make the blueberry puree as warm as the beurre blanc. The timing of this dish is important. Everything should be ready to go just before the beurre blanc is made. Because it is a delicate sauce you want to make sure it does not break.

LOBSTER THERMIDOR

(2 servings)

INGREDIENTS:

2	each	quarter lobsters, shucked
1	tbsp	olive oil
1/2	cup	chopped scallions
1/2	cup	minced green bell peppers
1/2	cup	chopped mushrooms
2	tbsp	chopped fresh tarragon (or 1 tbsp dry)
1/4	tsp	black pepper
1/2	cup	lobster stock
1/4	cup	white wine
1/4	cup	brandy
1	tsp	Dijon mustard
1.5	cups	white sauce
1/2	cup	fresh grated parmesan cheese

PROCEDURE:

Follow the cooking method for sautéed lobster. Remove the meat from the body and claws, being careful to keep the body shell intact. Cut all the meat into small bite-sized pieces and set aside, reserving the tomalley in a seperate bowl. In a medium-sized sauté pan, heat olive oil over medium high heat. Add scallions, bell peppers, chopped mushrooms, tarragon and black pepper. Cook 2–3 min until vegetables just start to soften, then add brandy and wine and turn heat to high. When liquid is boiling, add lobster stock and reduce to almost a glaze. Lower heat to medium, add the white sauce and Dijon mustard, and blend thoroughly. Add the pieces of lobster and the tomalley and mix together. When mixture starts to bubble, remove from heat. Place mixture in shells, top with parmesan cheese and sprinkle with paprika. Set under a preheated broiler and brown. Serve immediately.

LOBSTER STIR-FRY

(4–6 servings)

Stir-frying is easy and fun and, most of all, delicious. All you need for equipment is a good deep skillet, a knife and a wooden spoon. If you have a Wok, that's even better, but don't feel you need one to do stir-frying because you don't. I have a Wok, but for years I just used a cast-iron skillet. Stir-frying is a method of cooking used by the Chinese for centuries and in the past 20 years or so it has gained great popularity, especially with people watching the amount of fat they take in. Stir-frying uses far less oil or fat than deep frying does, and as a result the food you prepare with this method is much healthier to eat.

INGREDIENTS:

3	tbsp	peanut oil
1	tbsp	minced garlic
1	tbsp	minced ginger root
1	cup	julienne carrots
1	cup	julienne onions
1	cup	broccoli florets
1	cup	julienne celery
1	cup	sliced green onions
1/2	cup	water chestnuts
1	cup	snow peas
1	cup	whole mushrooms
1	lb	lobster meat
1	cup	fresh bean sprouts
1	tsp	black pepper
2	tbsp	soy sauce

Thickening sauce

1/4	cup	cooking sherry
1	tsp	sugar
1	tbsp	corn starch
4	tbsp	cold lobster stock or water

115

PROCEDURE:

For the best results use raw lobster meat. Follow the directions in the cooking method section for sautéed lobster. Mix all ingredients for thickening sauce in a small bowl and set aside. Preheat a large skillet or wok over high heat, add oil and when oil is hot add garlic and ginger root. When garlic turns golden brown add carrots, onions, celery, broccoli, green onions and water chestnuts. Toss frequently and cook 2–3 min until vegetables start to soften. Then add snow peas and mushrooms and cook another 2 min. Add soy sauce and black pepper and mix. In the center of the skillet or wok clear a space so the pan is exposed. Pour in the thickening sauce and when sauce begins to bubble and thicken add lobster and bean sprouts and cook another 2 min. Toss entire mixture until completely blended and cover for 1–2 min or until lobster is completely cooked but not overdone. Serve over Chinese noodles, fried rice or plain.

Note: You can vary this recipe quite a bit, by adding shrimp, scallops, oysters, squid and whole clams. Any combination of seafood only enhances the dish.

LOBSTER FRIED RICE

(6–8 servings)

This is an easy dish to make and I love it, even when I am not preparing Chinese food. It does, however, embellish any Oriental dish you are preparing. And it will last several days after preparation.

INGREDIENTS:

2	tbsp	peanut oil
2	tbsp	clarified butter
1	tbsp	minced garlic
1	tbsp	minced ginger root
1/2	cup	chopped carrots
1	cup	minced onions
1	cup	minced celery
1	cup	chopped scallions
1/2	cup	sliced water chestnuts
1	tsp	black pepper
4	tsp	soy sauce
1	tsp	Gravy Master
2	cups	brown rice
3.5	cups	chicken stock, boiling hot
1	lb	cooked lobster meat, bite-sized pieces
3	each	eggs, scrambled
1	cup	bean sprouts
1	tsp	Worcestershire sauce

PROCEDURE:

In a large skillet, heat oil and butter until hot. Add garlic and ginger root and cook until golden brown (do not let burn). Then immediately add carrots, onions, celery, chestnuts and scallions. Cook on medium-high heat 5–7 min, stirring constantly. Add rice to mixture and stir for 2–3 min until rice starts to crackle. Add chicken stock, soy sauce and Gravy Master, and stir so that all rice is free from the bottom of the pan. Reduce heat to simmer, cover and cook for 20 min. Remove cover and toss in lobster meat, scrambled eggs and

117

bean sprouts. Shut heat off, add 1 tsp of soy sauce and the Worcestershire sauce, and cover for 1–2 min. Serve.

Note: You may vary this recipe in a couple of different ways. If you want a stronger lobster taste use lobster stock in place of the chicken stock. You can delete the soy sauce and the Gravy Master and the rice will be a lot lighter in color. If you do not want any Oriental taste, delete the ginger. Once cool, place in covered plastic container and refrigerate. Rice will last 3 or 4 days with no problems if properly refrigerated.

LOBSTER LINGUINE
WITH PESTO

(4–6 servings)

INGREDIENTS:

2	fluid oz	clarified butter
1	each	large shallot, minced
1/2	cup	olive oil
4	cups	sliced mushrooms
1/2	tsp	black pepper
4	1–2 lb	lobsters cooked and shucked
2	cups	diced tomatoes
1	cup	pesto sauce (see *Sauces*)
1/3	cup	cooking sherry
1	cup	freshly grated parmesan cheese
1/4	cup	finely chopped parsley
2	lbs	cooked linguine

PROCEDURE:

In a large saute pan, put clarified butter on high heat until butter begins to smoke. Add shallots and cook until brown, about 1 min. Pour in olive oil and add mushrooms. Keeping heat on high, cook until mushrooms start to brown and water begins to escape from them. While mushrooms are cooking cut lobster into bite-sized pieces and place all tomalley and roe in a bowl. Add the lobster to the pan and toss as you cook. Add the tomatoes, pesto, tomalley and sherry. Continue to cook and toss for about 2–3 min to make sure all ingredients have combined. Reduce heat and simmer 1–2 min. Remove from heat. Preheat broiler in oven. Set a half pound of linguine on each plate and top with lobster mixture, sprinkle parmesan cheese on top and broil until cheese melts, top with chopped parsley, place plate on an underliner plate and serve.

LOBSTER EGG ROLLS

(2 dozen)

Even though egg rolls can be made from crepes, I have had much more success with commercially prepared dough that is cut into 3–4 in. squares. This Won Ton wrap is available at almost every supermarket and it comes both fresh and frozen.

INGREDIENTS:

1	lb	freshly shucked lobster meat
1	lb	uncooked ground pork, very lean
1	cup	finely chopped mushrooms
1/4	cup	finely chopped celery
1/2	head	finely chopped bok-choy (Chinese cabbage)
1	cup	sliced scallions
1	tsp	chopped garlic
1/4	cup	cooking sherry
2	tbsp	fresh grated ginger root
1/2	cup	minced green pepper
1	tbsp	soy sauce
1/2	cup	finely chopped water chestnuts
2	tbsp	Hoi Sin sauce
1/2	tsp	Five-spice powder
1/2	tsp	black pepper
1/2	cup	water
3	tbsp	cornstarch
24	each	egg roll wrappers
1	qt	frying oil (rapeseed or canola preferred)

PROCEDURE:

In a large bowl mix all ingredients except water, cornstarch and wrappers. In a small bowl using a fork mix water and cornstarch until smooth. Place wrappers on flat working area, brush entire surface of wrapper with cornstarch mixture. Place 1/4 cup of lobster filling in center of wrapper and carefully roll wrappers around filling. Fold all corners in tight and brush again with cornstarch. Heat oil in wok or frying pan to 350°F. Fry egg rolls, 4 or 5 at a time, in hot oil until golden, or 4-6 min, turning constantly. Drain on paper towels and serve immediately.

DEVILED LOBSTER CASSEROLE

(4 servings)

This recipe is quick and delicious. There are several recipes for deviled lobster; this one is mine.

INGREDIENTS:

1	lb	freshly shucked lobster meat
1/2	cup	chopped green pepper
1/2	cup	chooped celery
1/2	cup	chopped onions
1/3	cup	chopped scallions
1/4	cup	chopped parsley
1-3/4	cup	crushed Ritz crackers
1	tsp	Dijon mustard
1/2	tsp	black pepper
1/4	cup	sherry
1/4	cup	all purpose cream
3/4	cup	clarified butter
		Tabasco sauce

PROCEDURE:

In a large mixing bowl combine green peppers, celery, onions, scallions, and parsley. Cut lobster meat into chunks and add it to the mixture. Add 1-1/2 cups of the crushed crackers, the mustard, pepper, a couple dashes of Tabasco, cream, sherry, and 1/2 cup of clarified butter. Mix thoroughly with a wooden spoon. Butter the inside of a 1-1/2 qt casserole dish and place mixture inside it. Cover with the remaining cracker crumbs evenly over the top. Drizzle the rest of the clarified butter over the cracker crumbs. Place casserole dish in preheated oven at 350°F for 30 min or until cracker crumbs turn golden brown. Remove from heat and serve immediately.

121

LOBSTER AMERICANO

(2 servings)

This is my own version of the classic dish, Lobster *a l'Americaine*. I usually cook these one at a time, but if you have a large enough sauté pan you can cook them both together, as described here. A very impressive-looking dish when completed, not to mention the mouth-watering aroma that permeates the area.

INGREDIENTS:

2	1–2 lb	lobsters
2	tbsp	olive oil
2	tsp	minced garlic
1/4	cup	minced onions
1/2	cup	minced celery
2	each	medium size tomatoes, skinned and diced
1/4	tsp	black pepper
1	dash	Worcestershire sauce
1	dash	tabasco
1/2	cup	white wine
1/4	tsp	Old Bay seasoning
2	cups	cooked brown rice
1/4	cup	chopped parsley

PROCEDURE:

First immerse the lobsters into a rapidly boiling pot of water for 1 min to kill them. Remove from water, lay them on their back and cut them in half lengthwise with a chef knife. The intestinal track which runs down the back of the tail section and the stomach should be removed. Save the tomalley and the roe, if any, to add later on. In a large sauté pan or skillet, preferably 12", place olive oil and garlic. On high heat cook until garlic starts to brown. Immediately add the onions, celery, spices, worcestershire and tabasco. Cook for about 2 min. Add lobster tomalley and roe to pan and stir into mixture. Add lobsters split side down ; sprinkle tomatoes over the lobsters and add white wine. Cover and saute on medium heat for 8–10 min. Place 1 cup of rice each on a large lipped plate or shallow bowl, remove lobsters from pan and place split side up on top of rice. Cover with sauce, sprinkle with parsley and serve.

This dish can also be served on pasta. If you do use pasta, I suggest a very fine one, like angel hair.

Note: if you object to boiling or steaming a live lobster to kill it there are humane alternatives. You can kill a lobster almost instantly if you plunge the point of a knife into its head between the eyes, or sever the spinal cord by flipping the lobster on its back and making an incision where the tail and chest are connected.

LOBSTER DIAVOLO

(2 servings)

This is the Italian version of the classic dish Lobster *a l'Americaine.*

INGREDIENTS:

2	1–2 lb	lobsters
4	tbsp	olive oil
2	tsp	minced garlic
1/2	cup	minced onion
1/2	cup	minced celery
1/2	cup	minced green pepper
1/4	cup	chopped parsley
1/4	tsp	black pepper
1	dash	tabasco
1	dash	Worcestershire sauce
1/2	tsp	oregano
1/2	tsp	basil
2	each	medium size tomatoes, skinned and diced
1/2	cup	marsala
1	lb	cooked pasta
1/4	cup	parmesan cheese

PROCEDURE:

Immerse the lobsters in hot water to kill them, just as in the recipe for Lobster Americano. Remove from water, lay them on their backs and cut them in half lengthwise with a chef knife. The intestinal tract which runs down the back of the tail section and the stomach should be removed. Save the tomalley and the roe if any to add later on.

In a large saute pan or skillet, preferably 12", place olive oil and garlic. Cook on high heat until garlic starts to brown. Add the onions, celery, peppers, parsley, pepper, tabasco, Worcestershire, oregano and basil. Cook over medium heat for 4-5 min, then add lobsters split-side down. Pour the tomatoes, marsala wine, tomalley and roe (if any) over lobsters, cover and cook on medium heat 8–10 min. On a large lipped plate or shallow bowl place 8 oz. of the pasta. Remove lobsters from pan and place split side up on pasta, cover with sauce, sprinkle with parmesan cheese and serve.

I like angel hair pasta with this type of dish; linguine is also very good. Some versions of this recipe call for serving the lobster on a rice ring, also a very nice presentation. Arrange the rice on the plate in a ring and place the lobster in the center of the ring. Make sure all the sauce goes inside the ring.

Note: if you object to boiling or steaming a live lobster to kill it, there are humane alternatives. You can kill a lobster almost instantly if you plunge the point of a knife into its head between the eyes, or sever the spinal cord by flipping the lobster on its back and making an incision where the tail and chest are connected.

LOBSTER KENNEBUNK

(4 servings)

When I was living in Boston I once ate at Locke Ober, one of Boston's oldest and most prestigious restaurants. That was where I first saw a lobster with its outer shell carved out. The name of the dish was Lobster Savannah. I made this dish up using the same technique. This particular dish is extremely attractive and, boy, can you have fun with it. When I cooked it for some friends of mine in Kennebunkport who are hardcore boiled lobster fans, they were swayed just a tad from their downeast syndrome. They loved it!

INGREDIENTS:

4	1–2 lb	lobsters
2	tbsp	roux
1	cup	all-purpose cream
1	tbsp	Dijon mustard
1	tbsp	clarified butter
1	clove	minced shallot
1/2	cup	minced celery
1/2	cup	chopped scallions
1/2	cup	chopped red bell pepper
1	clove	minced garlic
2	oz	brandy
3	oz	lobster fumet
2	dash	tabasco
2	dash	white wine Worcestershire sauce
1/4	tsp	black pepper
1/2	tsp	leaf thyme
1	cup	grated gruyere cheese

PROCEDURE:

The lobsters are going to be boiled, but with a slight variation of the normal procedure. Using either metal or wooden skewers; run the skewer down the inside of the body and tail of the lobster, and tie firmly to the tail with butchers twine. This is keep the lobster tail stiff

126

and straight while it cooks. If this was not done the lobster tail will curl: for this particular recipe we need the the body and tail straight because the finished product is going to sit on the plate with the tail sticking straight out. Follow the usual procedure for boiling lobsters. After lobsters are cooked, set them aside to cool and assemble the rest of the ingredients.

When lobsters are cool enough to handle, remove skewer and string and place upright on work area. Remove both claws from body and set aside. With a sharp boning knife pierce the shell, starting about an inch behind the eyes, and carve an opening down to the tip of the tail, exposing the tail meat and the tomalley. On a select lobster the opening should be 4" to 5" long and 1-1/2" wide. Remove tail meat, tomalley, and coral (if any) and set aside. Shuck the claws and slice the claw meat and the tail meat into bite-sized chunks.

 In a small saucepan on medium heat bring cream to a boil and add roux, whip briskly with wire whip and, when sauce starts to thicken, add Dijon mustard (this will make it very thick, which is good).

In a medium-sized pan on high heat place clarified butter and shallots. When shallots start to brown, add celery, bell peppers, garlic and scallions. Cook until other vegetables start to brown (3 min). Add the worcestershire and tabasco, turn heat down to medium and cook 1 min, then add the brandy. Once the alcohol has evaporated add the fumet. Bring to a boil and add black pepper, leaf thyme and chunks of lobster meat, tomalley and coral. Cook about 1 min and then add the dijon cream sauce. Mix thoroughly and remove from heat.

Using a large serving spoon place lobster mixture into the cavity you created in the lobster body. Top mixture with thinly grated gruyere cheese and place lobsters on baking sheet. Preheat oven to 450°F and bake lobsters for 8–10 min. Remove from oven and serve.

Variations: You can really use any type of swiss cheese. I prefer gruyere because it is dryer. You can also use onions instead of scallions. If you like, add a few sauteed mushrooms to the top of the mixture before you top it with the cheese.

This dish can be prepared well ahead of time, in the morning for example, and refrigerated. If you do this there is two ways to do it. One, do not put the mixture into the shell until just before you bake it. Put both the lobster bodies and the mix in the refrigerator and assemble later. Two, assemble the lobsters and cover with plastic film or foil. Either way is perfectly acceptable. Just remember: when you bake them increase the cooking time 4 min.

GRAM RUTH'S LOBSTER PIE

(4 servings)

There are many recipes for lobster pie. Some are individual servings like this one; others are whole pies which you would serve in slices. My grandmother has been making this one for over 50 years. She is now 89 and still making it. It is a simple and quick casserole pie that gets rave reviews at the dinner table. I know because when I visit my Grandmother, a native of the Granite state, she prepares this dish and I love it. So in honor of her I would like to share this recipe with you.

INGREDIENTS:

1	2-lb	lobster cooked and shucked, or
		8 oz of lobster meat
2	tbsp	butter
1/4	cup	sherry
3	tbsp	butter
1	tbsp	flour
3/4	cup	light cream
2	each	egg yolks

PROCEDURE:

In a small saucepan melt 2 tbsp of butter, add sherry and boil for 1 min. Slice the cooked lobster meat into bite-sized pieces and add to saucepan. In a small double boiler on high heat melt 3 tbsp of butter and add. Blend thoroughly to make a roux. Using a wire whisk, slowly add the cream and the coral (if any) and juices from the lobster. When sauce has thickened and become smooth remove from heat. Whisk the egg yolks into the sauce and return to heat for 3 min. Add the lobster mixture to the sauce and place into individual casserole dishes and cover with cracker crumb topping (see next page). Bake at 350°F for 10–12 min.

Cracker Crumb Topping

3/4	cup	crushed Ritz crackers
1/4	cup	crushed potato chips, homemade if possible
1/4	tsp	paprika
2	tsp	grated parmesan cheese
1	tbsp	sherry
2	tbsp	melted butter

Mix all dry ingredients in a bowl, then add wet ingredients and blend thoroughly. There is a variation to this topping which I use quite often. When preparing the topping follow the same recipe but add to the wet ingredients 1 tbsp of lobster tomalley.

LOBSTER PALIZZOLO

(4 servings)

This is lobster ravioli with herb butter. Italians are famous for creating pasta dishes using lobster. I'm not Italian but my best friend is, and I have enjoyed many a good pasta dish at his house. So, Billy, I named this dish after you and your family, and will share it with everyone.

INGREDIENTS:

Pasta

1	ea	egg
3	ea	egg yolks
2	tbsp	water
1	tsp	olive oil
1/4	tsp	salt
1-3/4	cup	flour

In a mixing bowl combine egg, egg yolks, water, salt and oil and blend thoroughly. In a large bowl place 1-1/2 cups flour, make a hole in the center and add egg mixture, and mix well with wooden fork. Place the rest of the flour on the a flat work counter and knead dough until smooth. Cover with plastic wrap and refrigerate while you prepare the filling.

Filling

1	lb	fresh shucked lobster meat, chopped
1/4	lb	ricotta cheese
1/4	lb	softened cream cheese
1/4	tsp	fresh squeezed lemon juice
1/8	tsp	black pepper
1	ea	egg
1	ea	egg yolk, well beaten
		salt and pepper to taste

Combine first five ingredients into a mixing bowl, add eggs and blend thoroughly. Set aside.

Herb Butter

1/2	lb	salted butter
1	tbsp	chopped garlic
1/4	cup	chopped parsley
1/4	cup	fresh chopped basil
1/4	cup	fresh chopped oregano
1/4	cup	fresh chopped lemon thyme
1/4	tsp	black pepper
1/4	tsp	Worcestershire sauce

Melt butter in saute pan add garlic and cook until garlic starts to brown. Add rest of ingredients and blend together. Keep on low heat until ready to serve.

PROCEDURE:

To assemble ravioli: Cut pasta in half. Flour a clean work surface, place one part of the divided pasta on floured work surface and roll into thin large rectangle, about 1/8" thick. Using a teaspoon, drop filling on pasta about 2-1/2" apart. Using a pastry brush moisten all pasta aound the filling. Roll remaining dough to the same-size rectangle and place over the one with the filling. Gently press the two sheets of pasta together between filling. With a raviloi cutter cut into individual squares. Brush the cut edges with an egg wash to hold them together.

Place ravioli into boiling water and cook 6–8 min. Drain and place them on dishes. Top with hot herb butter and parmesan cheese. Serve immediately.

LOBSTER PAPILLOTE

(4 servings)

This particular method of cooking is like poaching under pressure. What you are doing is forming a pouch that, when heated, creates steam and cooks the lobster under a small amount of pressure. The bouquet you experience when you first open the hot pouch is truly a sensation. The vegetables are crisp and the lobster meat is very tender.

INGREDIENTS:

1/4	lb	whole butter
1	cup	julienne red bell peppers
1	cup	julienne yellow bell peppers
1	cup	sliced leeks
1/2	cup	sliced red cabbage
1	cup	whole mushrooms
1	cup	artichoke hearts, cut in half
1	cup	small broccoli florets
1/2	cup	dry white wine
1	tsp	black pepper
1/2	cup	fresh chopped basil
1/2	cup	fresh chopped Italian parsley
4	tbsp	bread crumbs
1-1/2	lbs	raw lobster meat (use method 6)
1	cup	court bouillon
8	pieces	heavy aluminum foil 12 x 12"

PROCEDURE:

In a large skillet melt butter over medium high heat and add peppers, leeks, red cabbage, broccoli, mushrooms and wine. Cook for 2–3 min until vegetables start to soften. Then add artichoke hearts, black pepper, basil and parsley and blend thoroughly. Cook 1 min more and remove from heat.

To assemble papillotes, place 4 of the pieces of foil on a flat work surface and evenly distribute the raw lobster onto all 4 pieces. Cover each portion of lobster

133

with an even amount of the vegetable mixture, then pour 1/4 cup of court bouillon over the top of them. Sprinkle 1 tbsp of bread crumbs over the vegetables and place another piece of foil over the top. Tightly seal both pieces of foil together so that no leakage will occur. Place finished papillotes on a baking sheet and put in preheated oven at 500°F. Cook 4–5 min until the papillotes have puffed way up. Remove from heat, transfer to plates and serve immediately.

LOBSTER TARRAGON

(4 servings)

This dish is served chilled. It can be made ahead of time, and is great for entertaining on a hot summer's night.

INGREDIENTS:

1	tbsp	chopped tarragon, fresh if possible
4	each	quarter lobsters
2	cups	cooked crabmeat
1	tsp	Dijon mustard
1	cup	mayonaise
1	tbsp	tomato paste
1	tbsp	lemon juice
1/2	tsp	black pepper

PROCEDURE:

Boil lobsters, cool, remove meat from lobsters and save the shells. Keep the tail intact by cutting only the underside of the shell to remove the meat. Chop all the lobster meat and combine with all the other ingredients. Mix thoroughly, put back into shells and refrigerate until you are ready to serve.

LOBSTER NEWBURG

(4 servings)

Every year on Christmas eve the traditional holiday dinner for our family has been Lobster Newberg, with delmonico potatoes and an array of festive vegetables—my favorite meal.

There is quite a bit of history to this particular recipe. It first appeared in print in 1895, but it was made famous about 20 years earlier. In 1876 a West Indies sea captain named Ben Wenberg brought the recipe to Charles Ranhofer, chef at Delmonico's restaurant in New York. Called "lobster *à la* Delmonico," the dish was an overnight success. Charles Delmonico, the owner, later changed it to "lobster *à la* Wenberg."

One day Delmonico and Wenberg got into a squabble and Delmonico took it off the menu. But popular demand forced him to restore it, so he did but named it "lobster *à la* Newberg," reversing the first three letters of Wenberg's name. Now, a century later, the dish can be found in restaurants all over the United States and around the world. It is a delicious dish and one that always makes a statement at the dinner table.

INGREDIENTS:

1	qt	milk
1/2	lb	margarine
1	cup	flour
1		finely minced shallot
2	fluid oz	clarified butter
4	1–2 lb	lobsters, cooked and shucked; save tomalley
1	tsp	white wine Worcestershire sauce
1	tsp	black pepper
1/2	cup	sherry
2	tbsp	paprika
1/2	cup	lobster fumet
1		patty shell *(voul-au-vent)* per person

PROCEDURE:

First make a white sauce. In a 2-qt double boiler bring 1 qt of milk to 180°F. While the milk is heating, melt the margarine in a small saucepan. When the margarine is totally melted, add the flour and mix thoroughly with a wire whip. Slowly add this roux to the scalded milk, stirring constantly with the whip. The sauce will thicken; keep whipping to avoid lumping. Add the Dijon mustard mix and then the lobster fumet, slowly whipping until smooth. Set aside. (This sauce has less cholesterol than the traditional sauce made from cream and egg yolks.)

In a large sauté pan put the clarified butter and the minced shallot and cook on low heat until the shallot is slightly browned. Cut the lobster meat into bite-sized pieces and add to butter and shallots. Cook on high heat for about 1 min, then add worcestershire and black pepper. Stirring constantly with a wooden spoon, add the sherry and the lobster tomalley and cook until the sherry starts to boil, or about 2 min. Sprinkle in the paprika and add the white sauce. Reduce heat and simmer for 2 min. Remove from heat and serve on a golden brown patty shell.

Note: The Newburg can be refrigerated for up to four days. Place in a plastic storage container and allow to cool thoroughly before covering tightly.

LOBSTER ALFREDO

(4–6 servings)

This is a very rich Italian dish, best served on Fettucine pasta, but it can be served with any pasta.

INGREDIENTS:

1/2	cup	lobster fumet
1	cup	fresh shucked lobster meat
1 1/4	cups	freshly grated parmesan cheese
1	tbsp	whole butter
4	each	egg yolks
1	dash	Worcestershire sauce
1	tsp	Dijon mustard
1/4	tsp	Tabasco
1/4	tsp	black pepper
2	cups	heavy cream
1/4	cup	fresh chopped parsley
3/4	lb	fettucine pasta

PROCEDURE:

In a medium-size sauce pan, over medium heat, melt the whole butter and add the lobster fumet and the heavy cream and turn heat up to medium high. When cream is hot, just before boiling add the parmesan cheese and whisk briskly until all the cheese is melted and dissolved into the cream. Add the Worcestershire, tobasco, black pepper and Dijon and whisk thoroughly again. Reduce heat again to a fast simmer and allow mixture to simmer 20 min. While the sauce is simmering, cook the pasta to the "doneness" you prefer, drain and set onto plates. Cut the lobster meat into very small pieces and add to sauce, add the egg yolks and turn heat to medium high. The sauce should be of medium thickness—the more you cook the egg yolks the thicker it will become. Ladle sauce over pasta, sprinkle with fresh chopped parsley and serve.

LOBSTER AND SHRIMP BOLOGNESE

(4–6 servings)

INGREDIENTS:

1	tbsp	chopped garlic
1/4	cup	infused olive oil, rosemary and garlic
12	ea	headless U12 shrimp, peeled, deveined and butterflied
1	lb	fresh shucked lobster meat
1/3	cup	julienne carrots
1/3	cup	slivered leeks, white end only
1/3	cup	chopped broccoli
1/2	cup	strips of yellow, red and green peppers, 1/4" thick, 2" long
1/3	cup	cut cauliflower
1/3	cup	red cabbage
1/3	cup	Madeira wine
1	tbsp	fresh chopped assorted herbs, rosemary, basil, thyme, tarragon
4	cups	cooked bowtie pasta *(see next page)*
1	cup	saffron shrimp sauce *(see next page)*

PROCEDURE:

Heat 12" sauté pan over medium high heat, add olive oil and garlic. When garlic just starts to brown, add shrimp and wine. Brown shrimp on both sides then add all vegetables except tomatoes and chopped herbs, Sauté for 3–4 min until veggies are "al dente." Add tomatoes and shrimp stock, cook 1 min more. While mixture is cooking, place hot bowtie pasta on the plates and distribute evenly. Top all the pasta with vegetable and shrimp mixture. Ladle saffron shrimp sauce over the top of the dish, garnish and serve immediately. I like to serve this dish with crispy French bread and a nice chilled bottle of dry white wine. Bon appetit!

139

Saffron Shrimp Sauce

In 2-qt sauce pan place 1 1/2 qt of water and the shells from the shrimp. Add 1/4 tsp of sea salt, and 1 healthy pinch of saffron. Bring stock to a boil and then turn down to a slow boilf for 45 min. Strain off shells and bring stock to a full boil again. Mix 1/2 cup arrowroot and 1/4 of water together until it is a smooth paste. Add paste to boiling stock and whip with a wire whisk until smooth. Add 1/2 cup heavy cream and let sit while you prepare main dish.

Cooking Pasta

In a 4-qt sauce pan, bring to a boil 2 qts of water and then add 1 tbsp of oil and 1 tsp of sea salt. Add pasta and cook until "al dente," about 8–9 min. Strain and serve.

LOBSTER CAPELLINI

(4–6 servings)

This is a great dish for two people. It is also served well as either an appetizer or an entree. It is an inexpensive dish to prepare and easy to make. All the ingredients are readily available at your local supermarket.

INGREDIENTS:

2	tbsp	olive oil
1	tsp	fresh chopped garlic
1/4	lb	Crimini mushrooms, sliced
1/4	lb	Shitake mushrooms, stems removed and sliced
1/4	tsp	black pepper
1/4	cup	lobster stock
1/4	cup	Madiera wine
1/4	tsp	Worcestershire sauce
4	ea	large basil leaves, chopped
8	ea	artichoke hearts, sliced
1	tbsp	chopped oregano
1	cup	chopped scallions
2	cups	chopped tomatoes
1	lb	fresh shucked-lobster meat
2	tsp	grated Parmesan cheese
4	ea	scallion flowers, for garnish
4	each	fresh basil leaves, for garnish
1	lb	capellini
1	gal	water
1/2	tsp	salt

PROCEDURE:

In an 8–10-qt pot, add water and salt and bring to a boil. Add capellini and cook for 8–10 min. In a 10" sauté pan or skillet, over medium-high heat, heat olive oil and garlic until garlic is golden brown. Be very careful not to burn garlic. Add all mushrooms and sauté until half cooked, then add pepper, lobster stock, Madiera wine and Worcerstershire. Toss ingredients with wooden spoon and add basil, artichoke hearts, toma-

141

toes, lobster and scallions. Reduce heat and simmer for 2–3 min while draining pasta.

Remove pasta from water and drain completely. Rinse pasta with warm water and place pasta on plates into evenly divided portions. Top each plate of pasta with the lobster sauce, garnish with fresh basil leaves and scallion flowers, sprinkle with Parmesan cheese and serve. Bon Appetit!

Note: This dish can be prepared ahead of time. I suggest you precook the pasta, and then to reheat it, just lower the pasta into a pot of boiling water for 1 min. The sauce can easily be heated in the same-size pan in 5–7 min.

CRAB CAKES WITH LOBSTER AND ROASTED RED PEPPERS

(eight 2-oz cakes)

INGREDIENTS:

12	oz	snow crab
3	dash	tobasco
1	tsp	Old Bay seasoning
1	each	eggyolk
1/8	tsp	black pepper
1	tsp	chopped garlic
1/4	tsp	onion powder
2	tbsp	mayonnaise
1	tsp	lemon juice
1	tsp	paprika
1	cup	bread crumbs
4	ea	lobster claws, chopped
1/2	cup	olive oil
1/2	cup	cocktail sauce *(see recipe below)*

PROCEDURE:

In a medium-size bowl mix the mayonnaise with the crab meat, egg, lemon, and all spices. Use a spoon to blend thoroughly. Add the bread crumbs and use your hands to mash the bread crumbs into the crab mix until they are stiff, the consistency of meatballs. Portion out eight 2-ounce balls of the mix, then flatten the shape the cakes into half-patties or cakes.

Put the olive oil in a medium-size skillet or sauté pan on medium high heat. When oil is hot (4–5 minutes) place the cakes in oil and fry on each side until golden brown. Remove cakes from pan and place them on paper towels to remove excess oil. Transfer to plates and serve with cocktail sauce or roasted red pepper sauce.

Cocktail sauce

1	ea	10-oz jar of Heinz Chili Sauce
1/4	tsp	horseradish
1/8	tsp	black pepper
1	tbsp	fresh squeezed lemon juice

In a small bowl, mix all the ingredients together and serve, or store until needed. This recipe can be made one or two days ahead of time.

LOBSTER FUSILLE

(4–6 servings)

This is a great pasta dish. It is easy to prepare in less than 25 min, and those who eat it will savor the flavor and relish the fact that it is low in calories and fat.

INGREDIENTS:

1	lb	fresh shucked-lobster meat
1	tbsp	olive oil
1	ea	large red onion
1	tbsp	chopped garlic
1	rib	celery, chopped
1	cup	freshly cut vine-ripened tomatoes
1	tbsp	tomato paste
1/2	cup	scallions
1/4	tsp	oregano, dry
1/4	tsp	basil, dry
1/2	tsp	crushed red pepper
1/2	cup	black olives, sliced
1/4	cup	chopped parsley
8	oz	fusille pasta

PROCEDURE:

In a large sauté pan, over medium heat, heat the oil, add the onion, celery, and garlic, and cook for 6–7 min until vegetables are firm but cooked. While this is cooking, cook your pasta in a large pot of boiling water.

Add the tomatoes, herbs and red pepper. Stir mixture and add tomato paste, scallions, lobster and black olives and mix thoroughly. Once pasta is cooked, drain it and add it to the mixture and toss. Sprinkle with chopped parsley and serve.

CHICKEN AND LOBSTER SAUTE´ WITH GRAPES

INGREDIENTS:

8	oz	chicken cutlets
8	oz	fresh shucked lobster meat
1/2	tsp	fresh ground black pepper
1/4	tsp	rosemary, chopped fresh or dry
1/4	tsp	thyme, fresh or chopped
1	tbsp	olive oil
1/2	cup	chicken broth
2	tsp	corn starch
1	tsp	lemon juice
12	ea	large seedless green grapes
12	ea	large seedless red grapes
3	tbsp	Madeira wine or sweet sherry

garnish: lemon, fresh rosemary and radicchio

PROCEDURE:

Cut the chicken into julienne strips about 1/2" wide. In a small bowl, place the chicken and lobster meat and sprinkle with the fresh herbs, salt and pepper. In a large nonstick sauté pan or skillet, warm the oil over medium to high heat until hot but not smoking. Add the chicken and lobster mixture and sauté for 5 min. Transfer to the dinner plate.

In a small bowl, blend the Madeira wine and the corn starch. Return pan to heat and add chicken broth and grapes. Sauté until grapes are hot and chicken broth starts to bubble. Add the Madeira wine and corn starch mixture until sauce thickens, about 1 min. Spoon the sauce over the chicken and lobster, garnish and serve immediately. Bon appetit!

146

CREAMED SPINACH WITH LOBSTER ON LINGUINE

(4 servings)

INGREDIENTS:

1	tbsp	olive oil
1	tbsp	minced garlic
1/2	cup	chopped scallions
3/4	cup	sherry
1/4	cup	lobster fumet
1/4	tsp	fresh thyme
8	oz	chopped lobster meat
2	tsp	cornstarch
1/2	cup	buttermilk
2	tbsp	sour cream
1/4	cup	chopped fresh parsley
1/4	tsp	Red Hot sauce
1	8oz	bag of spinach, cooked and chopped
8	oz	linguine
1/4	cup	chopped walnuts
1/4	cup	parmesan cheese

PROCEDURE:

In a large 8-qt stock pot fill with water and boil. Cook the pasta until "al dente." In a large sauté pan heat the oil and add garlic and scallions, cook until scallions are soft, being careful not to burn the garlic. Stir in the sherry, thyme, and fumet. Add the lobster, buttermilk and sour cream. Blend the cornstarch with 2 tbsp of water and add to mixture to tighten the sauce. Add the spinach, walnuts and parmesan cheese. Portion mixture over pasta, sprinkle with chopped parsley, and serve.

♥♥♥♥♥♥♥♥♥♥

Stuffed Entrees

BASIC LOBSTER STUFFING

(4 servings)

This is my basic lobster stuffing; it can be used in many different ways. It is very versatile and makes many different things taste great.

INGREDIENTS:

6	oz	lobster meat, chopped
2	tbsp	lobster tomalley
1⁄2	lb	crushed Ritz crackers
1⁄2	cup	grated parmesan cheese
3	oz	sherry
1⁄4	tsp	black pepper
1⁄4	tsp	celery salt
1⁄4	tsp	garlic salt
1	dash	Tobasco sauce
1⁄2	cup	clarified butter or olive oil

PROCEDURE:

In a food processor using the knife attachment, place the cooked meat of one quarter lobster. Turn motor on and run until finely chopped. Remove lobster and do the same to the Ritz crackers. In a medium-sized bowl combine all ingredients and mix thoroughly.

This stuffing can be refrigerated and will last several days if properly covered. Store in a sealed plastic container.

Note: In most of my recipes I use a 1-1⁄4 lb lobster, called a "quarter." A quarter lobster yields between 5 and 6 oz of fresh shucked meat.

BAKED STUFFED SHRIMP

(4 servings)

INGREDIENTS:

20		U-15 jumbo gulf shrimp
2	cups	lobster stuffing
1	cup	clarified butter

PROCEDURE:

Preheat oven to 400°F. Peel and devein shrimp, leaving the tail and the last section of the shell intact on each shrimp. In indivual casserole dishes arrange five shrimp in each dish with tails sticking upwards, with the meat of the shrimp butterflied and resting on the bottom of the dish. Carefully cover the shrimp with the stuffing, leaving only the tail of each shrimp exposed. Drizzle 1 oz of clarified butter over the stuffing of each dish and then bake for 12–15 min. Remove from oven and serve immediately with the remaining clarifed butter and lemon.

Note: The "U-15" is the size of the shrimp: it means that one pound of this size will give you 15 shrimp. Shrimp come in a variety of sizes, but this one is considered a good one to cook with. If you use a smaller shrimp, cook them a little bit less.

BAKED STUFFED LOBSTER

(2 servings)

INGREDIENTS:

2	2 lb	lobsters
2	cups	basic lobster stuffing
4	oz	sea scallops, sliced
2	oz	clarified butter (drawn butter)

PROCEDURE:

Follow the cooking method for a baked stuffed lobster. After cutting and cleaning the lobster and prepping it for stuffing, place 2 oz of scallops in the body of each lobster. Fill the rest of the body and the tail section with the basic lobster stuffing, and drizzle with the butter. Place the lobsters on a baking sheet and brush the entire body with clarified butter, then put the lobsters in a preheated oven at 375°F and bake for 18–20 min. Remove from heat and serve immediately with drawn butter and lemon. Other items may be used to embellish the flavor of this dish: instead of scallops, try oysters, smoked salmon, crabmeat, mussels or shrimp.

Note: If you are using a convection oven, reduce oven temperature to 325°F and cook for 12–15 min. I like the two-pound lobster the best for this recipe. All sizes may be used; just be careful how long you cook them.

BAKED STUFFED SCALLOPS

(4 servings)

INGREDIENTS:

2	lbs	fresh scallops
2	cups	basic stuffing
1/2	cup	clarified butter

PROCEDURE:

In each shell place 8 oz of fresh scallops. If you are using large, random-sized sea scallops, you might consider cutting them into a uniform size. This insures that all the scallops are cooked the same. Cover each shell of scallops with 1/2 cup of stuffing and then evenly drizzle 2 oz of butter over each. Place in a preheated oven at 400°F for 12–15 min. Remove from heat and serve immediately with freshly squeezed lemon juice.

The best way to serve these is in a large scallop or coquille shell, if you can find them. Most gourmet shops carry them. If not, use individual casserole dishes.

BAKED STUFFED SALMON WITH LOBSTER BEURRE BLANC

(4 servings)

INGREDIENTS:

4	8-oz	fresh salmon fillets
1	cup	basic stuffing
1/4	cup	clarified butter
1	cup	lobster beurre blanc (see *Sauces*)

PROCEDURE:

Using a sharp knife, fillet each side of a salmon and cut into 8-oz fillets. If you are purchasing the fish already filleted I suggest you order the tail section. There is nothing better for salmon eating then a nice, thick juicy tail piece. Lay each fillet on a countertop and using a sharp fillet knife slice the fillet in half length-wise. Fill with 1/4 cup of stuffing and then brush with clarified butter. Place in preheated oven at 400°F for 12–15 min. Remove from heat and top each fillet with 1/4 cup of the lobster beurre sauce. Serve immediately.

BAKED STUFFED SWORDFISH

(4 servings)

INGREDIENTS:

4	6–8 oz	swordfish steaks
1	cup	basic stuffing
1	cup	hollandaise
1/4	cup	finely chopped parsley

PROCEDURE:

Using a sharp fillet knife slice the fish lengthwise right up to the skin but do not cut all the way through. Fill the incision with 1/4 cup of stuffing per steak. Place on a greased baking pan and put into an oven preheated to 400°F. Bake for 12–5 min, remove from heat and top with hollandaise and chopped parsley. This dish may also be grilled.

BAKED STUFFED TUNA

(4 servings)

INGREDIENTS:

4		6–8 oz tuna fillets
1	cup	basic lobster stuffing
1	cup	green peppercorn sauce
1/4	cup	chopped parsley
1/4	cup	chopped scallions, white part only
1	dash	paprika

PROCEDURE:

Using a sharp fillet knife, slice the fish in half lengthwise to the skin, but not all the way through. Fill the incision with 1/4 cup of lobster stuffing per steak. Place on a greased baking pan and put in preheated oven at 400°F. Bake for 12–15 min, remove from heat and top with sauce, scallions and parsley. Sprinkle with paprika and serve.

BAKED STUFFED MUSHROOMS

(yield 2 dozen)

These were a favorite at every cocktail party my parents had when I was growing up. They are easy to make; I know that for a fact because I have made them from the age of nine on, and I'm still making them.

INGREDIENTS:

1	cup	vegetable oil
24	large	mushroom caps
24	pieces	lobster knuckles
2	cups	basic stuffing

PROCEDURE:

Put oil in a large shallow pan and heat on medium high heat. When oil is hot, add washed mushrooms caps. Cook until soft on the outside, but still firm on the inside. Remove from oil and pat dry on paper towels. When cool enough to handle, put one lobster knuckle in the center of each cap, top the rest of the cap with the stuffing and place on a baking sheet. Put in a preheated oven at 400°F for 10 min. Remove from heat and serve.

Note: if you don't have knuckle meat, any part of the lobster will do as well.

BAKED STUFFED ZUCCHINI

(4 servings)

These are absolutely wonderful, especially in the summer months, when the zucchini is fresh from local gardens.

INGREDIENTS:

1.5	lbs	freshly shucked lobster meat
4	each	medium-size zucchini
2	cups	basic lobster stuffing
1	cup	clarified butter

PROCEDURE:

Cut the ends off each zucchini and slice it in half lengthwise. Using a teaspoon hollow out the seeded section, creating a zucchini boat. Brush each half zucchini with clarified butter. Cut the lobster into bite-size chunks and distribute evenly among all eight zucchini boats. Cover each of them with stuffing and drizzle the remaining butter over all of them. Place them in a shallow baking dish and put them in a preheated oven at 375°F. Cook for 15–20 min or until the top of the stuffing is golden brown. Remove from heat and serve immediately.

Crepe Entrees

LOBSTER CREPES

Crepes are not a new form of preparing and serving food, but rather a very old way that has become popular in the last 20 years or so. *Crepe* is a French word for a very thin pancake. Being a peasant food, crepes are found in many different countries, not just France. Each nationality has its own version but they are all made with basically the same ingredients. For example, in Israel they are called blintzes, in China they are Won Ton or egg rolls, in Mexico they are enchiladas, in Italy they are cannelloni, and in Hungary they are palacsintas.

I have had a lot of fun preparing crepes and I enjoy serving them because of the excitement my guests show for eating them. Crepes make a great lunch or brunch item. They are easy to make and can be prepared well ahead of time.

Basically crepe batter is a thin pancake batter made up of flour, eggs, milk and oil. There are two methods for preparing crepes: using an upside-down pan or the traditional way in an upright pan. For simplicity I am going to describe the traditional way.

BASIC CREPE BATTER

(30–35 crepes)

INGREDIENTS:

4	each	eggs
2	cups	flour
2-1/4	cups	milk
1	dash	salt
1/4	cup	clarified butter or oil

PROCEDURE:

In a medium-sized mixing bowl and using electric beaters, beat eggs to a light frothy yellow. Combine salt and flour and add to eggs. Blend thoroughly. Slowly add milk, beating constantly. When ingredients are well blended, add oil or butter. Pour batter through a sieve and refrigerate for one hour before using.

You can purchase many types of pans to make crepes but it is really not necessary. A good aluminum or stainless steel omelet pan or sauté pan works just fine. I use an aluminum 8" sauté pan by choice and it works great!

Preheat pan over medium heat and lightly coat with cooking oil. Wipe excess oil out of pan. Now you are ready to cook the crepes. The key to cooking crepes is having a well-seasoned pan and finding the correct cooking temperature so that the crepes come out golden brown. All it takes is some practice. Don't get upset if you loose a few crepes in the process. I have, and so has everyone who has made them.

Using a 2-oz ladle, ladle the batter into the pan while slowly orbiting the pan so that batter covers the bottom of the pan evenly. Place pan on stove and cook crepe until it starts to bubble. Using a wooden spatula or spoon, lift crepe and check to see if it is golden in color. They usually take about one minute to cook. Lift crepe from pan and place on paper towels until cool and then stack. Keep crepes covered so they do not dry out. After you cook each crepe, lightly season the pan again with oil. I recommend using a kitchen cloth moistened with oil. Use the kitchen cloth after each crepe is made.

In all the recipes for crepes I use freshly shucked lobster meat. Using the hot boiled cooking method yields the best results. Crepes are a great way to use any leftover lobster you might have. If you buy the meat already shucked they are also a great way to present them.

LOBSTER DIVAN CREPES

(4 servings)

INGREDIENTS:

8	each	crepes
1	lb	freshly shucked lobster meat
8	spears	cooked broccoli (crisp)
2	cups	divan sauce *(see next page)*
2	cups	grated sharp cheddar cheese

PROCEDURE:

In individual shallow baking dishes place a crepe and assemble each crepe in the following manner: Place about 2 oz of lobster in the center of each crepe and then place the broccoli with the flower end sticking out of each crepe over the lobster. Using a 1-oz ladle pour 1 oz of divan sauce over lobster and broccoli.

Fold the crepe over into a cylindrical shape and repeat the process until all four baking dishes have two complete crepes in them. Cover the center of the crepes with divan sauce and then with 1/2 cup of grated cheese per baking dish. Place in preheated oven at 350°F for 15–20 min. Remove from heat and serve immediately.

Divan sauce

1/4	cup	butter or margarine
1/4	cup	flour
1	cup	milk
1	cup	sour cream
1	tsp	Worcestershire sauce
1	tsp	Dijon mustard
2	tbsp	lobster tomalley *(optional)*
1	cup	grated sharp cheddar cheese

In a saucepan over medium heat, melt butter. Then stir in flour and blend thoroughly. When it starts to bubble, slowly add milk, using a wire whisk. When all the milk is added and sauce is thick, add sour cream, Worcestershire, mustard and tomalley. When sauce is thin and smooth, add grated cheese and blend thoroughly.

LOBSTER NEWBURG CREPES

(4 servings of 2 crepes each)

INGREDIENTS:

8	each	crepes
4	cups	white sauce
1	each	finely minced shallot
2	fluid oz	clarified butter
4	1-2 lb	lobsters, cooked and shucked (save tomalley)
1	tsp	white wine Worcestershire sauce
1	tsp	black pepper
1/2	cup	sherry
2	tbsp	paprika
1/2	cup	lobster fumet

PROCEDURE:

In a large sauté pan place the clarified butter and the minced shallot and cook on low heat until shallot is slightly browned. Cut the lobster meat into bite-sized pieces and add to butter and shallots. Cook on high heat for about 1 min then add Worcestershire sauce and black pepper. Stirring constantly with a wooden spoon, add the sherry and the lobster tomalley and cook until the sherry starts to boil, about 2 min. Sprinkle in the paprika and add the white sauce, reduce heat and simmer for 2 min. Turn heat down and keep warm.

One crepe at a time, place crepe cooked-side down on large dinner plate. Using a 2-oz ladle, place 2 oz of newburg in center of crepe and fold ends of crepe over. Place another crepe right beside the first one and repeat the process. When both crepes are assembled, pour 1 oz of sauce over the center of the two crepes and serve.

LOBSTER FLORENTINE CREPES

(4 servings of 2 crepes each)

INGREDIENTS:

8	each	crepes
1	lb	freshly shucked lobster meat
1/4	cup	clarified butter
1/4	cup	minced onions
1/2	cup	sliced mushrooms
1	tsp	chopped garlic
1/4	cup	chopped walnuts
1/4	tsp	black pepper
1	tsp	fresh squeezed lemon juice
1	cup	cooked spinach, well drained
1/2	cup	white sauce
1	cup	Hollandaise sauce
1/4	cup	fresh chopped parsley

PROCEDURE:

In a medium-sized saucepan over medium heat, heat butter and add garlic, onions and mushrooms. Saute until soft. Add walnuts, black pepper, lemon, spinach and white sauce. Blend thoroughly and remove from heat.

In individual shallow baking dishes assemble crepes. Place 2 oz of lobster in each crepe, top with spinach mixture, and wrap each crepe. Place two in each baking dish, folded side down. Bake in preheated oven at 350°F for 10 min.

While crepes are baking make Hollandaise sauce (see *Sauces*).

Remove crepes from oven, top with Hollandaise, garnish with chopped parsley and paprika and serve.

LOBSTER DIJONESE CREPES

(4 servings of 2 crepes each)

INGREDIENTS:

8	each	crepes
1	lb	freshly shucked lobster meat
1/4	cup	clarified butter or substitute
1	tbsp	finely chopped shallots
2	cups	sliced mushrooms
1/4	tsp	Worcestershire sauce
1	dash	Tabasco sauce
1/4	tsp	black pepper
1/4	cup	lobster fumet *(optional)*
1/2	cup	white wine
1-1/2	cups	white sauce
2	tbsp	Dijon mustard
1/4	cup	chopped parsley

PROCEDURE:

In a medium-sized saucepan over medium high heat, bring butter to the point that it almost starts to smoke. Add shallots; when they start to brown, add mushrooms, Worcestershire sauce, Tabasco, pepper, fumet and white wine. Bring to a boil and then simmer for 10 min, stirring occasionally. Slice lobster into bite size pieces add to mixture along with the mustard, and cook another 2–3 min. Add white sauce and half of the parsley. Simmer 5 min more. Assemble crepes on warm dinner plates. Placing one crepe at a time on plate cooked side down place mixture in center and fold crepe over. Repeat procedure with second crepe, cover top of crepes with reserve sauce and remaining parsley. Serve immediately.

LOBSTER AND ARTICHOKE CREPES

(4 servings of 2 each)

INGREDIENTS:

8	each	crepes
1	lb	freshly shucked lobster meat, cut into chunks
1/4	cup	clarified butter
1	tbsp	finely chopped shallots
1/4	cup	lobster fumet
1	tbsp	lobster tomalley *(optional)*
1/2	cup	white wine
16	each	canned artichoke hearts, well drained
1-1/2	cups	white sauce
3/4	cups	freshly grated parmesan cheese
1/4	tsp	black pepper
1	dash	Tabasco sauce
1/4	cup	Ritz cracker crumbs

PROCEDURE:

In a medium-sized saucepan heat butter until it almost smokes. Add shallots and cook until brown. Add fumet, tomalley and white wine, and reduce liquid to one half the original amount. Add artichoke hearts, white sauce, cheese, pepper and Tabasco sauce, and blend thoroughly. Add lobster. Reduce heat to a simmer and simmer 5 min.

Assemble crepes in individual baking dishes. With the cooked side of the crepe down, fill each crepe with 2–3 oz of the mixture and fold the crepes closed. Cover the center with the leftover sauce and sprinkle with the cracker crumbs. Place baking dishes in preheated oven at 350°F for 10–12 min. Remove from heat and serve immediately.

LOBSTER THERMIDOR CREPES

(4 servings of 2 each)

INGREDIENTS:

8	each	crepes
2	each	2-lb lobsters, cooked and shucked
1	tbsp	olive oil
1/2	cup	chopped scallions
1/2	cup	minced green bell peppers
1/2	cup	chopped mushrooms
2	tbsp	chopped fresh tarragon (or 1 tbsp dry)
1/4	tsp	black pepper
1/2	cup	lobster stock
1/4	cup	white wine
1/4	cup	brandy
1	tsp	Dijon mustard
1-1/2	cups	white sauce
1/2	cup	fresh grated parmesan cheese

PROCEDURE:

Follow the cooking method for preparing a sautéed lobster. Remove the meat from the body and claws, being careful to keep the body shell intact. Cut all the meat into small bite-sized pieces and set aside, reserving the tomalley in a separate bowl.

In a medium-sized sauté pan, heat olive oil over medium high heat, add scallions, bell peppers, chopped mushrooms, tarragon and black pepper. Cook 2–3 min until vegetables just start to soften, then add brandy and wine and turn heat to high when liquid is boiling. Add lobster stock and reduce almost to a glaze. Lower heat to medium and add the white sauce and Dijon mustard and blend thoroughly. Add the pieces of lobster and the tomalley and mix together. When mixture starts to bubble, remove from heat.

Assemble crepes in individual baking dishes. Place one crepe at a time in baking dish with the cooked side down. Fill each crepe with 2–3 oz of mixture and fold. When each baking dish is complete, cover the center of the crepes with the remaining sauce and then top with cracker crumbs. Place in preheated oven at 350°F for 10–12 min. Serve immediately.

LOBSTER PALACSINTAS

(4 servings of 2 each)

This is the Hungarian version of the French crepe. This dish is deep fried. I have had great success with rapeseed oil. This is the best oil to use for frying: a cousin of the soybean, it is very light, the lowest in saturated fat, and contains no cholesterol.

INGREDIENTS:

8	each	crepes
1	lb	freshly shucked lobster meat
2	cups	grated Swiss cheese
1/4	tsp	black pepper
1/2	tsp	flour
12	each	eggs, well beaten
2	cups	seasoned bread crumbs
1	tbsp	paprika
1	cup	country mustard sauce *(see next page)*
1	qt	frying oil

PROCEDURE:

Pat lobster dry so there is no excess liquid on it. Chop lobster into very small pieces and in a small bowl mix with the grated swiss cheese. Add flour and toss until completely blended. Lay crepes, cooked side down, on a flat counter top. You are going to fold these crepes like an envelope so that all corners are sealed. You do not want any of the cheese mixture to be exposed to the frying oil, so it is essential that each crepe is sealed properly. Do not over fill crepes with cheese and lobster mixture. Brush the entire surface of the crepe with the egg. Place enough of the mixture in the center of each crepe, and then flatten out mixture so the thickness of each crepe will be consistent. Fold corners over the sides and top and then brush all seals with egg. When you are certain all seals are tight dip entire

174

crepe in beaten egg and then in bread crumbs. Then do it again. All crepes should be double dipped in egg, then in bread crumbs. In a large frying pan place oil and heat to 350°F. Place crepes in pan and fry on all sides until crepes are golden brown. Remove crepes from oil and place on paper towels to drain excess fat. Serve immediately with mustard sauce for dipping.

Country Mustard Sauce

1/3	cup	mayonaise
1/3	cup	creamy Dijon mustard
1/3	cup	whole grain mustard
1/4	tsp	Worcestershire sauce
1	tsp	fresh squeezed lemon juice
1	tbsp	white wine

In a small bowl mix all ingredients.

CREPES WITH LOBSTER AND GREEN TOMATO FILLING

(4 servings)

INGREDIENTS:

Crepes

1 1/2	cups	whole milk
3	ea	eggs
2	tbsp	butter, melted
1	cup	all-purpose flour
1/2	tsp	salt

Lobster and Green Tomato Filling

3	ea	medium-size green tomatoes, sliced
1/2	lb	fresh shucked-lobster meat
1	tbsp	olive oil
1/2	tsp	chopped garlic
4	ea	basil leaves, chopped

PROCEDURE:

In a medium-size mixing bowl combine milk, eggs, and butter and whisk till blended, then add flour and salt and beat until smooth. Refrigerate for 1 hr before making crepes.

To make crepes, season a 7" or 8" skillet or sauté pan. Heat pan until a drop of water skitters. Melt 1 tsp of butter and then pour enough batter into pan to just cover the bottom, usually about 2 oz. Tip and twirl the pan so that the bottom is completely covered evenly. (The trick is to discover exactly how much batter this takes.) The batter should set immediately using medium to medium-high heat. When the edges of the crepe appear to be dry, flip the crepes over in the pan, then cook for about 20 sec more.

176

In a medium-size sauté pan or skillet, over medium-high heat, add the olive oil and garlic. When garlic starts to brown, add the tomatoes and lobster, then sauté for 1–2 min until tomatoes start to soften. Add the basil and then sauté for 1 min more. Remove the pan from the heat and then place crepes, browned sides down, on plates. Arrange filling in center of each crepe. Then fold sides of crepe over, garnish and serve.

Dishes with Lobster

SALMON AND LOBSTER ALFALFA

(4 servings)

This is a healthy dish that is really tasty. If you are watching your cholesterol this is a dish you will absolutely fall in love with.

INGREDIENTS:

3	cups	water
1	cup	white wine
4		4-oz salmon fillets (skin removed)
4	oz	cooked lobster meat
1	cup	skim milk
1	tsp	Dijon mustard
1	tbsp	chopped chives or scallions
1/4	tsp	black pepper
1	tsp	lime juice
3	tsp	horseradish
1	tbsp	cornstarch
4		asparagus tips (one per serving)
2	tsp	chopped parsley
4	tufts	alfalfa sprouts
1	dash	paprika

PROCEDURE:

In a shallow pan, bring water and wine to a boil. Place salmon fillets and asparagus in pan and poach 6–8 min. Remove salmon and asparagus from water, pat dry and place on a plate.

While salmon is poaching, in a small saucepan add milk, cornstarch, chives and black pepper. On medium high heat and stirring constantly with a wire whip, bring mixture to a bubbling state until sauce thickens (about 2 min). Remove from heat and add horseradish and lime juice, then return to heat for 1 min, stirring briskly.

Slice asparagus tips in half lengthwise and place both

halves on top of the salmon. Then add 1 oz of lobster per dish. Distribute sauce evenly over each of the four pieces of salmon, then top with a small tuft of alfalfa sprouts. Sprinkle chopped parsley and paprika over alfalfa, garnish and serve.

CHICKEN ELIZABETH

(4 servings)

This recipe is very special to me because I named it after my mother, in her loving memory. Her passion for cooking inspired me to take it up as my profession. I learned a lot from her and her joy of cooking became mine.

She also had a great love for the sea. We always had a boat and we spent a lot of time as a family on the water. I have vivid memories of childhood summers, of checking the tides early in the morning so we could plan our day. Dead low tide was the time we would go clamming. We always got some lobstering in, and at the end of the day we would stop at a local farmstand to get fresh vegetables for dinner.

This particular dish was my house speciality in several country inns. It has been requested by national food magazines, newpapers and authors of other cookbooks. It is really quite simple to prepare and a glorious dish to eat. This is the original, but don't be surprised if you see it on a menu; it has been copied many times.

INGREDIENTS:

4	6 oz	boned and skinned chicken breasts
2	1 lb	lobsters, shucked (save tomalley)
4	tsp	lobster tomalley
4	sq	puff pastry 5 x 5 in.
1	cup	Hollandaise sauce (see *Sauces*)
1	each	egg
1/2	cup	water

PROCEDURE:

On a flat surface place chicken breasts between two pieces of clear plastic film or wrap. Pound gently with a meat-tenderizing mallet. Lay breasts with inside of breast facing up, spread 1 tsp of tomalley over the

183

inside of each breast. Sprinkle with black pepper and then in the center of each breast place 2 oz of lobster meat cut into chunks. Roll the chicken breasts into a small log shape with the split sealed tight to contain the lobster.

Roll out puff pastry to 1/8 in. thick. Place rolled chicken in center of puff pastry with the folded seam facing up. Wrap puff pastry around chicken like an envelope. Trim off excess dough and place trimmed side down on a greased baking sheet.

Beat egg and water together to make egg wash and lightly brush each Elizabeth. This will make the crust shine when it is done. Place in preheated oven at 400°F and cook for 20–25 min, until crust is golden brown. While cooking make Hollandaise sauce. Remove from heat, top with Hollandaise, and serve immediately.

Note: If you do not know how to make puff pastry it can be purchased at your local supermarket, in the freezer section. You can also substitute Bearnaise sauce in place of Hollandaise.

BEEF OSCAR

(4 servings)

INGREDIENTS:

4		6-oz center-cut tenderloins of beef (filet mignon)
1/4	cup	clarified butter
1/4	cup	brandy or cognac
1/2	lb	cooked lobster meat
12	each	cooked asparagus tips, cut 3 in. long
1	cup	Bearnaise sauce (see *Sauces*)

PROCEDURE:

Season the beef with salt and pepper. In a medium-sized skillet heat butter over medium high heat. Butterfly the filets of beef so you can later stuff them with the lobster. Place the filets of beef into skillet along with the brandy and cook to your desired temperature. When done on both sides remove from heat and stuff center of beef with lobster. Place beef onto plates and top with the asparagus, and then cover them with Bearnaise sauce. Serve immediately.

SALMON OSCAR

(4 servings)

INGREDIENTS:

1/2	lb	cooked lobster meat
4		8-oz fresh salmon fillets
12		cooked asparagus tips, cut 3 in. long
1	cup	Bearnaise sauce (see *Sauces*)
1	qt	court bouillon (see *Soups,* etc.)

PROCEDURE:

Bring bouillon to a boil in a pan made for poaching. Add salmon fillets to the boiling bouillon. Cook until done, 5–7 min. Remove and pat salmon dry. Place salmon on individual plates, and top with 2 oz of lobster meat each. Then cover with Bearnaise sauce. Serve immediately.

VEAL OSCAR

INGREDIENTS:

1/2	lb	cooked lobster
1	lb	escalopes of veal
1/2	cup	flour
6		eggs, well beaten
1	cup	clarified butter
1/2	cup	white wine
12		cooked asparagus tips, cut 3" long
1	cup	Bearnaise sauce (see *Sauces*)

PROCEDURE:

Gently pound the escalopes of veal into small medallions. Dip the medallions of veal into the flour, then the egg, and coat well. In a large saute pan heat butter. Place egg-dipped veal into hot butter and cook on both sides until lightly golden. Add wine and cook 1 min more. Remove veal from heat, drain on paper towels and distribute evenly onto dinner plates. Top with asparagus and then cover with Bearnaise sauce. Serve immediately.

With all the Oscar dishes I heat the lobster meat and the cooked asparagus in the microwave just enough to warm them up. If you heat them to mush the lobster will get very tough. If you don't have a microwave, have a little poaching water hot on the stove to give them a small bath just before serving. I also like my asparagus crunchy. It gives great texture to the dish. You can substitute broccoli if asparagus is not in season. These dishes are easy to prepare and very elegant to serve.

ABOUT THE AUTHOR

Brian Coffey is a chef, writer, scuba diver, fisherman, sportsman, and a relentless explorer, finding new and exciting interests on his road through life. He has published recipes in several cookbooks and national food magazines. He has taught cooking classes in several country inns in New England. He was born in Nashua, New Hampshire in 1953. When he was two his family moved to Plymouth, Massachusetts, and soon after to Hanover, Massachusetts.

Spending every summer at a beach house in Marshfield, Massachusetts, Brian acquired a passion for the sea. At fourteen he became a scuba diver and discovered an even greater passion for the world under the sea. Brian started cooking at the early age of nine, and has been in the hospitality and restaurant business ever since.

After working in several successful restaurants in Boston, Brian moved to the White Mountains of New Hampshire. He worked many years as an executive chef in country inns in the Mount Washington Valley, and now resides in Conway, New Hampshire. His love for the lobster and its presentation is seen daily in his specialities.

Look for these other fine books from
Douglas Charles Press and Covered Bridge Press

*New England Women of Substance: Fifteen Who Made a
Difference*   J. North Conway $12.95

The Boston Dictionary
              John Powers, illus. by Peter Wallace $10.95

Fenway: An Unexpurgated History of the Boston Red Sox
                          Peter Golenbock $15.95

New England Wild Places
                          Michael J. Tougias $12.95

True New England Mysteries, Ghosts, Crimes and Oddities
                          Charles T. Robinson $12.95

The New England Ghost Files
                          Charles T. Robinson $14.95

The New England Ghost Files (Cassette)
                          Read by Joseph A. Citro $ 9.95

*Until I Have No Country: A Novel of King Philip's War in
New England*   Michael J. Tougias $12.95

*How to Blow Up Animals: A Beginner's Guide to Fun With
Balloons*   Lon Cerel $ 9.95

*The Man Who Talked to Trees... and More Strange New
England Tales*   Curt Norris $12.95

New England's Most Sensational Murders
                          Marc Songini $10.95

New England Town Affairs
                          Charles J. Lincoln $12.95

Visions: Cape Cod and the Vineyard
                          Harold Wilson $ 9.95

New England's Best Family Getaways
                          Dan & Roberta LaPlante $14.95

Magnificent Mainers
                    Jeff Hollingsworth $14.95

Yankee Wildlife
                    Hilbert R. Siegler $12.95

Vampire Legends of Rhode Island
                    Christopher Rondina $ 9.95

Yankee Cinderella
                    Thomas B. Smith $12.95

The Sparrowhook Curse
                    Robin Moore $12.95

The Boston Bogeyman ... and More New England Mysteries
                    Curt Norris $10.95

The Rhode Island Dictionary
          Mark Patinkin, illus. by Don Bousquet $ 8.95

The Rhode Island Handbook
          Mark Patinkin, illus. by Don Bousquet $ 9.95

One Percent Inspiration, 99% Desperation
                    Mark Patinkin $19.95

A Pride of Lions: Joshua Chamberlain and Other Maine
Civil War Heroes   Willian Lemke $14.95

Return of the Downeast Detectiove
                    Karen Lemke $ 9.95

Mr. Spooner's in the Well ... and Other Massachusetts
Mysteries   Curt Norris $10.95

The Streamlined Double Decker Bus
                    Brownie Macintosh $ 9.95

A Workingman Skiff
                    William Campbell $ 9.95

A Workingman Skiff (Cassette)
                    Read by Salty Brine $ 9.95

The Quahog Stops Here
Don Bousquet $ 8.95

Quahogs are a Girl's Best Friend
Don Bousquet $ 9.95

Quahog State of Mind
Don Bousquet $10.95

A Rhode Island Album
Don Bousquet $24.95

Charlie Hall's Ocean State Follies
Charlie Hall $10.95

Harry Fig's Boston
Peter Wallace $ 7.95

Clean & Quiet: The Guide to Electric Powered Flight
Bob Aberle $12.95

Days Alive!
Edwin & Marjorie Lynn $14.95

The Boomer Book of the Dead
John J. Ronan $ 9.95

Please ask for these titles at your local bookstore first.

To order direct, send a check for the price of the book(s) plus $3.00 shipping and handling for the first book and $.50 for each additional book to:

Douglas Charles Press
440 Mendon Road
North Attleborough, MA 02760

Thank you for your patronage of
New England's Own Publisher!